The 500 Craziest WTF STATS

in Sports History

By

Peyton Bennett

Creator of WTF Stats™

ISBN: 9798365345256

INTRO

We're baaaack! If you read "The 400 Craziest WTF Stats in Sports History", welcome back! This edition includes over 100 new stats plus many of the other stats from the first book.

For those who are new to the brand, WTF Stats, welcome! Here you'll find the 500 CRAZIEST sports stats all complied into one book. You'll notice, that there's more NFL stats than other sports followed by MLB & NBA. It does not mean that there's more crazy NFL stats than other sports. Just like on our social media pages, we just favor the more popular American sports for no other reason than my own personal preference & what I find most interesting (selfish, I know). After years of scavenging the internet for the craziest sports stats that the WTF Stats community & myself could find, here's the top 500 craziest & most interesting ones. If you don't like it, now would be a great time to put this book down and find something else to entertain you during your bowel movement.

Since stats can change, if the date is not specified, then the stat is "as of now" when this book was written which was November 29th, 2022.

If you're looking for new or updated stats that weren't in the first book, just look for the ★. Enjoy!

CONTENTS

.

NFL STATS

1. **In his NFL career, Larry Fitzgerald had more tackles (41) than drops (30).**

This stat is one of my personal favorites and the craziest stat of all according to a tournament we held in 2020 on Instagram. Had to start the book with this one, but the rest will be in chronological order (kinda).

2. **7 different Packers QBs have led the NFL in passing yards since 1932. Aaron Rodgers is not one of them.** *

1998 - Brett Favre 4,212 yds
1995 - Brett Favre 4,413 yds
1989 - Don Majkowski 4,318 yds
1983 - Lynn Dickey 4,458 yds
1956 - Tobin Rote 2,203 yds
1944 - Irv Comp 1,159 yds
1942 - Cecil Isbell 2,021 yds
1941 - Cecil Isbell 1,479 yds
1936 - Arnie Herber 1,239 yds
1934 - Arnie Herber 799 yds
1932 - Arnie Herber 639 yds

3. **The Bears are the only NFL franchise to never have a QB throw 30 or more TD passes in season.** *

The most was 29 TD passes by Erik Kramer in 1995.

4. In 1943, not only did Sammy Baugh throw 4 TDs in a game, but he snagged 4 interceptions on defense in that same game.

Yep, don' think this will happen again.

5. During his 13-year career, Joe Namath only had 2 seasons where he had more TD passes than interceptions.

I know it was a different time, but I thought Joe Namath was a little better than that.

6. During the 1962 regular season, George Blanda threw 42 interceptions. There were only 14 games that season.

In terms of wins, this was still his best season as a starter (11-3). Pretty crazy for someone who played 26 seasons in the NFL. He played until he was 48!

7. While playing for the Eagles, Reggie White had more sacks (124) than games played (120).

Legendary stat for a legendary player

8. In 1974, there were 5 future Hall of Famers in the NFL Draft. The Steelers drafted 4 of them.

Lynn Swann (WR) - 1st round, 21st overall
Jack Lambert (LB) - 2nd round, 46th overall
John Stallworth (WR) - 4th round, 82nd overall
Mike Webster (C) - 5th round, 125th overall

The Steelers also signed Donnie Shell (after going undrafted in 1974) who was also inducted into the Hall of Fame.

The other Hall of Famer from this draft was TE Dave Casper who was picked 45th by the Raiders.

9. On 11/4/1979, the Seahawks finished a game with -7 yards of total offense (NFL record).

They lost 24-0 to the Rams. Seattle had 23 yards rushing & -30 net passing yards.

10. Brett Favre's first completed pass in his NFL career was to himself.

In week 2 of his 2nd NFL season, Brett Favre's first completed pass was batted at the line & reflected right back to him.

Bonus Stat: Brett Favre's first NFL pass attempt was a pick-six.

11. A wide receiver has never won the NFL MVP, but a kicker, Mark Moseley, won the award in 1982.

That season, he was 20 for 21 on FGs with a long of 48, and he was 16 of 19 on extra points. Not sure how he won MVP.

12. Jimmy Johnson won the AP NFL Coach of the Year despite being 7-9 that season.

Call me old fashioned, but I want a head coach's success to be measured by wins.

13. During the 1987 season that was shortened to 12 games, Jerry Rice had 22 receiving TDs while no other player had more than 11.

This is still the 2nd most receiving TDs in a season behind Randy Moss with 23 in 2007.

14. That same 12-game 1987 season, Reggie White had 21 sacks while no other player had more than 12.5.

The NFL record for sacks in a season is 22.5 by Michael Strahan (2001) & T.J. Watt (2021). Al 'Bubba' Baker had 23 sacks in his 1978 rookie season but the sack wasn't an official stat until 1982.

15. The last Browns head coach to win a game vs. the Patriots in Foxborough was Bill Belichick (10/25/1992).

Don't worry, this one won't change anytime soon.
Same ol browns.

16. The Buffalo Bills lost 4 straight Super Bowls (1990-1993).

Yeah, you probably already knew this one but that doesn't mean it isn't ridiculous. Just making it to the Super Bowl is tough enough (2/28 or 7.14% chance at the time). But to make it to FOUR in a row, and LOSE every single one. That's insane. Just to make it to 4 in a row is a 1/38,416 or .0026% chance. To lose all 4 is a 1/614,656 or .00016% chance.

17. Gale Gilbert is the only player in NFL history to go to 5 straight Super Bowls. He lost all 5.

Just read that again.

18. In 1994, Bucky Richardson once threw a completion and interception on the same play.

He threw a pass that was batted back to himself for a completion, then threw an interception. The defense declined the illegal forward pass penalty.

Here's the craziest part. This was the final pass of his NFL career.

19. Former QB Kim McQuilken's career NFL stats:

4 Pass TDs   29 INT

How he played 5 seasons & started 7 games I'll never understand. He had a career completion percentage of 39.7% and still won 2 games as a starter.

20. Chuck Howley won the Super Bowl MVP despite being on the losing team. He's the only player in NFL history to do this.

In Super Bowl V, OLB Chuck Howley had 2 interceptions & recovered a fumble.

21. Frank Reich set the record for the biggest comeback in NFL history AND NCAA history. He was a backup both times.

Yep, that's former Colts head coach Frank Reich. Down 31-0 at halftime of Orange Bowl, they subbed in Reich then won 42-40. AFC wild-card game, Reich started for the injured Jim Kelly. They were down 35-3, won 41-38 in OT.

22. Dan Marino has the NFL record for most consecutive pass attempts without being sacked (759). The next closest is 252 straight pass attempts (Mark Rypien).

252 isn't even a THIRD of 759. WTF

23. During the 1998 season, Derrick Thomas had 12 sacks. Half of them were in Week 1.

If he kept that 6-sack a game pace, he would have finished the season with 96 sacks.

24. In the 1999 draft, the Saints traded all of their 1999 picks & two of their 2000 picks (8 total) to Washington to draft Ricky Williams.

ALL OF THEIR 1999 PICKS. Like, not some of them, ALL of them. Plus a couple ones for the next season.

25. During the 1999 season, the Jaguars went 14-2 & lost in the AFC Championship. All 3 losses were to the Titans.

Really read that again. Maybe one of my favorite stats ever.

26. The 2000 Super Bowl champion Ravens had a 5-game stretch that season where their only points were Matt Stover FGs.

I mean they did lose 3 of those games, but how do you not score a single touchdown in the entire month of October & still win the Super Bowl!?

27. In 2002, the Texans beat the Steelers 24-6 but here's the crazy part...

Total yards: HOU:47   PIT:422

All 3 touchdowns scored by the Texans were on defense. Texans QB David Carr finished the game 3 for 10 with 33 yds passing while Steelers QB Tommy Maddox was 30 for 57 with 325 yds passing.

28. In 2002, Shaun Alexander scored 18 TDs. 28% of them came in the first half of one game.

For those who don't know how to math, that's 5 touchdowns in just 1 half of a football game.

29. In 2003, the Vikings had the 7th overall pick, but because time expired on them, they didn't pick until 9th.

I don't know if this qualifies as a stat, but it's hilarious and I had to include it in the book. Again, my book, my rules

30. Former OT Walter Jones was called for holding as many times as he made the Pro Bowl (9 times).

He also started all 180 of his career games.

31. Former Jets LT D'Brickashaw Ferguson played 10,755 out of a possible 10,756 snaps during his NFL career.

Never missed a game, never missed a start. The only play he missed was at the end of a game where they only had skill players out there to do multiple laterals.

Oh yeah, he also NEVER missed a practice.

32. Former NFL fullback, Larry Centers, has more career receptions (827) than Michael Irvin (750), Shannon Sharpe (815), & Chad Johnson (766).

A fullback! They don't even make those anymore.

33. On 9/12/04 Jerome Bettis had 5 carries for 1 yard & 3 TDs.

Classic weird stat right here.

34. Kurt Warner only played all 16 games during the season 3 times. All 3 times, he took his team to the Super Bowl.

Translation: If Kurt Warner started all 16 games for your team, you're going to the Super Bowl.

35. In 2006, LaDainian Tomlinson scored more points (198) than the Raiders (168).

Like not even just a little more, 18% more than an entire team! Granted, the Raiders did go 2-14 that season.

36. After going 14-2 during the 2006 regular season, the Chargers fired their head coach Marty Schottenheimer.

Yep this makes sense, 14-2 just isn't good enough.

37. In 2008, the Broncos had a 3 game lead in their division with 3 games left in the season. They missed the playoffs entirely.

Can't tell if this is more hilarious or sad.

38. On 10/18/2009, the Titans lost to the Patriots 59-0 & threw for a total of -7 yards.

Tom Brady was 29/34 with 380 yds & 6 pass TDs while Vince Young was 0/2 & Kerry Collins was 2/12 with -7 pass yds. Even Brian Hoyer was 9/11 with 52 yds. You would think the Titans had to play with a buttered potato or something but nope, they actually got to play with a real football just like the Patriots.

39. In 2011, Titans won more games (9) than they had rushing TDs (8).

I'm not sure exactly how often this has happened in NFL history, but I know it's not a lot. This could be the only time in recent years.

40. In 2010, the Chargers had the #1 ranked offense (YPG) & #1 ranked defense (YPG) yet didn't make the playoffs.

Probably the best 9-7 team to miss the playoffs in NFL history

41. In 2011, Percy Harvin had a 104-yard kick return that wasn't a TD. It's the longest non-TD play in NFL history.

Imagine running 104 yards just to get tackled right before the goal line.

42. In 2012, the Carolina Panthers lost their first 13 coin tosses. That's a 1/8,192 chance.

Best part is after losing 12 in a row, the Panthers asked their Facebook followers to vote if they should chose heads or tails for their next game, but that vote ended 50% to 50%.

43. In 2013, the Saints got 40 first downs in a game against the Cowboys.

Yes *that's an NFL record* and yes it probably has something to do with Drew Brees completing a lot of short passes.

44. On 12/8/2013, the Ravens were down 12-7 to the Vikings with 2:08 left in the game. The Ravens won 29-26 in regulation.

I wish I could describe in words how crazy this ending was, but you're better off going to this thing called the internet. It'll even show you video highlights!

45. During his playing career, linebacker Mike Vrabel had 10 receptions on offense. All 10 were touchdowns.

How does a linebacker catch 10 passes!? How are all 10 TDs!? Idk but he did have 14 targets and his longest reception was only 2 yards.

46. As a high school senior, Derrick Henry averaged 327.8 rushing yards & 4.2 rushing TDs per game.

Unless you're currently picking up your jaw from the floor, I don't think you understand how much 327 rushing yards PER GAME is. Those are passing numbers.

47. The Carolina Panthers have never had back-to-back winning seasons, but they still won the NFC South 3 years in a row (2013, 2014 & 2015)

Like never ever. Such a weird stat.

48. Ryan Fitzpatrick is the only QB in NFL history to have a game where he threw 6 TDs & 0 INT (11/30/14) AND have a game where he threw 0 TDs & 6 INT (9/25/16).

No QB is more deserving of this bizarre record than Fitzmagic himself. What a roller coaster of a career this man had.

49. Ryan Fitzpatrick started at QB for 9 different teams (NFL record) but didn't have a winning record with any of them. *

Team	Games Started	Record
Bills	53	20-33
Bengals	12	4-7-1
Dolphins	20	9-11
Jets	27	13-14
Rams	3	0-3
Buccaneers	10	4-6
Texans	12	6-6
Titans	11	3-6
Washington	1	0-1

50. Since 2013, every NFL team has had a tight end with 100 receiving yards in a game expect the Cardinals. They haven't had one since 1989.

Wow can't believe this stat is still true. Especially since the Cardinals got Zach Ertz.

51. During the entire 2014 season, the Chiefs didn't throw a single TD pass to a WR. (first time since 1964)

Well they sure made up for lost time once they got Mahomes.

52. Reggie Bush's final NFL season was 2016. He finished that season with -3 rushing yards.

Negative yards is always bad for a game, but for a season!?

53. In 2016, the Raiders committed 23 penalties for 200 yards in one game. Both are NFL records.

Hm that's weird. The Raiders are usually known for being so well-behaved and disciplined.

54. **During the 2016 regular season, the Patriots had more QBs start a game (3 - Tom Brady, Jimmy Garoppolo, & Jacoby Brissett) than total interceptions thrown (2).**

May be a little confusing to read, but this is absurd. Read it again if you have to.

55. **28-3**

Nothing else to explain here.

56. **In the 2018 season, the Chiefs averaged more points in their losses (36.2) than in their wins (34.3).**

Definitely can't blame the offense for their losses in 2018.

57. **The only player to catch a TD pass for the Bills in both 2018 & 2019, is offensive tackle Dion Dawkins.**

A lineman!

58. For 21 games in 2019-2020, the longest TD run by any Jacksonville Jaguar was 1 yard.

This is just so absurd. I still don't understand how this is possible. Not even a 2-yard TD run!?

59. On 9/20/20, the Falcons became the first team in NFL history to lose a game with 39 points & 0 turnovers.

Teams were 440-0 when scoring 39 points with 0 turnovers before that.
They also blew a 20-0 lead in that game.

60. In a high school PLAYOFF game, Will Grier threw for 837 yards & 10 TDs in a 104-80 win.

A PLAYOFF GAME!

61. Andy Dalton is the only NFL QB to start a season both 8-0 (2015) & 0-8 (2019).

I guess both are pretty impressive. Only 4 years apart too.

62. In their last game as a Seahawk, Kam Chancellor, Richard Sherman, & Earl Thomas all suffered a season-ending injury at the Cardinals' stadium.

Kam Chancellor suffered a neck injury & Richard Sherman blew out his achilles in their 2017 game in Arizona. The next season, Earl Thomas broke his leg on the same field.

63. The Buccaneers have won the NFC North* more recently than the Lions.

*It was called the NFC Central from 1967-2002 before the NFL split into 8 divisions.

64. Since 1969, there's been more Catholic Popes (5) than Steelers head coaches (3).

Uhhhhhhh yeah… pretty crazy stat huh?

65. To no surprise, Patrick Mahomes holds the NFL record for the most pass yards in his first 16 career starts (5,100 yds). The surprising part is who's 2nd on that list: Nick Mullens (4,405 yds).

I'm just surprised that Nick Mullens even has 16 career starts.

66. On Christmas 2021, Alvin Kamara tied the oldest single-game record in NFL history with 6 rushing TDs

Ernie Nevers rushed for 6 TDs on 11/29/1929.

67. Super Bowl LV was the first time in Patrick Mahomes' entire football career (high school, college & NFL) where his offense didn't score a single touchdown.

Translation: Patrick Mahomes is good at the football.

68. The first time during Josh Allen's life where the Bills won a playoff game, he was the starting QB.

He was 24 at the time.

69. Derrick Henry is the only human who has rushed for 2,000+ yards during a season in high school, college and the NFL.

Idk about non-humans though.

70. **For the 2020 season, if you only counted Derrick Henry's rushing yards from the 2nd half of games, he'd still have been 4th in the NFL in rushing yards.**

Really read that again. Pretty insane.

71. **In the 2020 season, Davante Adams had 17 Rec TDs. The Patriots had 8.**

That's more than double!

72. **Justin Tucker made 70 straight FGs from 40 yards or less before finally missing a 36 yarder in 2020.**

I don't care that you say, he's the best kicker of all-time.

73. **Chase Daniel has made $41,828,471 in his 13-year NFL career. ***

**5 starts ($8.3M per start)
8 TD passes ($5.2M per TD pass)
72 games ($580,951 per game played)
263 pass attempts ($159,044 per pass)**

Hmm maybe backup QB is the best job.

74. During his NFL career, Justin Tucker has never missed a FG in the final minute of regulation (17 for 17) or OT (5 for 5). *

The dude is just good at kicking footballs accurately. And far. And in the clutch.

75. Justin Tucker has made 65 straight FGs in the 4th quarter or OT. *

Streak is still going. I assume it'll never end & be in every edition of this book.

76. In the 2020 season, Deebo Samuel had more yards after catch (398) than receiving yards (391).

Lots of screens for Deebo.

77. Frank Gore played 16 seasons in the NFL & had exactly 16,000 career rushing yards with 100 total Tds.

81 Rushing TD
18 Rec TD
1 Fumble Recovery TD

78. During Adam Gase's tenure as the Jets head coach, they were 0-7 vs. WINLESS teams.

Couldn't even beat the teams that couldn't win.

79. Despite being 2nd, 3rd, & 4th on the all-time receiving yards list, Larry Fitzgerald, Terrell Owens, & Randy Moss never led the NFL in receiving yards in a season.

Writing a little bit extra under each stat is tougher than you think. I honestly don't know what to add here. Just enjoy the craziness of this stat and move along please. Thank you.

80. Only twice in NFL history has a team hosted 3 straight conference championships. Both teams were coached by Andy Reid.

02-04 Eagles
18-21 Chiefs (4 straight)

81. From 2012-2015, the Seahawks had the lead at least once in 70 straight games.

During the 2012-2015 seasons, the Seahawks were 46-18 in the regular season & 7-3 in the postseason with 2 Super Bowl appearances & 1 SB win.

82. Ray Lewis's first NFL sack was against Colts QB Jim Harbaugh and Ray Lewis's last NFL game was a Super Bowl win against head coach Jim Harbaugh.

Kind of a stat, but more just a cool full circle story.

83. The Harbaugh brothers (Jim & John) coached against each other in the f****** Super Bowl.

That deserved to be its own stat. What a cool moment for that family.

84. Not sure who's NFL passing stats are more impressive:

LaDainian Tomlinson		Mohamed Sanu
8	Completions	7
12	Attempts	8
143	Yards	233
7	TDs	4
0	INTs	0
146.9	QBR	158.3

85. The most recent number 1 overall pick to have a TD reception is OT Eric Fisher. There hasn't been another one since Keyshawn Johnson's last TD reception in 2006.

Still crazy that not even a QB taken 1 overall has a TD reception.

86. Both Peyton & Eli Manning retired with a career passer rating of 87.4 in the playoffs.

It's crazy cuz they're brothers.

87. Adam Vinatieri kicked in 51 different stadiums in his 24-year NFL career.

That's a lot of stadiums. But to really put into perspective how long he played in the league, he tackled Herschel Walker during his rookie season. He TACKLED him! Like by himself!

88. Drew Brees was never shutout in his entire NFL career as a starter. *

He started in 304 regular season & postseason games and his team scored in all 304 of them.

89. Aaron Rodgers has thrown 515 TD passes (incl. playoffs) during his NFL career. Marcedes Lewis is the only former first-round pick to ever catch a TD from Rodgers. *

You would think the Packers would just draft… never mind that's a crazy idea.

90. The first overall picks from 2017-2020 all tied in an NFL game before getting a win.

2017: Myles Garrett went 0-16 with the Browns in 2017, then tied with the Steelers in the first game of the 2018 season 21-21.
2018: Baker Mayfield, same tie as above

2019: Kyler Murray, tied first game of season 27-27 with the Lions
2020: Joe Burrow, Bengals lost first 2 games before tying with the Eagles 23-23 in Week 3.

91. Marques Colston is the Saints all-time leader in TDs scored (72), yet never made the Pro Bowl.

Let me reiterate that, Marques Colston never made the Pro Bowl! wtf

As of now (11/29/22), Alvin Kamara has 71 TDs.

92. In 2018, Josh Allen was drafted 7th overall & finished the season 6-10.

In 2019, Josh Allen was drafted 7th overall & finished the season 6-10.

In their first game against each other (2021), Josh Allen sacked Josh Allen. Josh Allen intercepted Josh Allen, and Josh Allen recovered a fumble from Josh Allen.

93. The Jets have never beaten the Eagles. Ever.

* Jets are 0-12 vs. the Eagles all time.

94. The Packers have NEVER won in Buffalo. *

They don't play much, but enough for the Packers to win at least once. Packers are 0-7 all-time in Buffalo

95. Since 2012, the Jaguars have spent $1.64 BILLION if free agency. No team has spent more yet the Jaguars still have the most losses since 2012. *

I guess you gotta overpay players to come lose in Jacksonville.

96. Julius Peppers retired with the same amount of career pick-6's as Champ Bailey (4).

In case you're unaware, Julius Peppers was a DE most of his career and Champ Bailey was one of the best CBs.

97. There have been more 1st round NFL draft picks in the Manning family than the entire state of Montana.

And I bet there's another Manning drafted in the first round before a player from Montana. Ryan Leaf is still the only one.

98. The Seahawks are the only NFL franchise that have never worn their white jerseys at home.

No idea the reasoning behind this or even if they're aware of this.

99. Steve Largent & Tyler Lockett are the only WRs in Seahawks history to record 3 consecutive 1,000 yard seasons. They both are under 6'0" & they were both born in Tulsa, OK on September 28th. *

How's that phrase about history repeating itself go again?

100. The Vikings & Ravens have played each other 7 times. Every year the Vikings win ('98, '09 & '17), they make it to the NFC Championship. Every year the Vikings lose ('01, '05, '13 & '21) they fire their head coach. *

So I guess this matchup of the only purple NFL teams is more important than we think. Can't wait until 2025!

101. The Arizona Cardinals have the longest title drought (since 1947) out of the 4 main professional sports. *

(MLB) Cleveland Guardians (FKA Indians): since 1948
(NBA) Sacremento Kings: since 1951
(NHL) Toronto Maple Leafs: since 1967

102. Ben Roethlisberger has attended more Super Bowl banner ceremonies (3) for the Patriots than he has for the Steelers (2).

Unlucky scheduling for Big Ben.

103. During the 2021 season, 100.69% of Rondale Moore's receiving yards came after the catch. *

He had 435 receiving yards & 438 YAC.

104. Eric Ebron's career rushing stats:
5 rushes   -6 yards   3 TDS

Nothing to explain here, just your normal rushing stats for a veteran tight end.

105. Peyton Manning & Trevor Lawrence are the only QB's to start their NFL career 0-9 on the road. They both got their first road win vs. the Chargers in week 3 of their 2nd season. *

These 2 former 1st overall picks that played college football in an orange #16 jersey sure do have a lot in common.

106. Patrick Surtain's last career TD was a pick-6 in Denver.
Patrick Surtain II's first career TD was a pick- 6 in Denver. *

Like father like son. Crazy thing is Patrick Surtain Sr. never even played for the Broncos.

107. Adrian Peterson is the only RB in NFL history to score a rushing TD for 6 different teams. *

Vikings, Cardinals, Washington, Lions, Titans, Seahawks

108.The game vs. the Bills on 12/26/2021 was the first time in Bill Belichick's head coaching career that he didn't force the opposing team to punt.

He had coached in 474 games prior (including playoffs).

109.In the year the former Raiders head coach John Madden passed away (2021), the Raiders won 6 games on the final play of the game. *

Most by any team since the 1970 merger.

110.During the 2021-22 season, the Raiders became the first team since at least 1940 with 10+ wins & a point differential of -50 or worse in same season. *

They finished the season 10-7 with a -65 point differential.

111.On 1/2/2022, the Giants finished the game with -6 passing yards as a team. *

For those wondering, sacks count as negative pass yards for team stats, but not individual stats.

112. **On 1/16/2022, Patrick Mahomes threw 5 TD passes in 10 minutes & 30 seconds of game time.** *

That's the fastest in postseason history.

113. **In the Divisional Round of the 2021-22 playoffs, the last play of regulation for ALL 4 games was a made FG.** *

Might go down as the best weekend of NFL Playoffs ever. Bengals beat the Titans, 49ers beat the Packers, Rams beat the Bucs, & Chiefs beat the Bills all with a wild finish.

114. **Only 2 QBs have won an FBS National Title & a Super Bowl as a starter. Both are named Joe.** *

Joe Namath & Joe Montana. Will Joe Burrow be the third..?

115. **As a rookie, Bengals kicker Evan McPherson had 3 postseason games with 4+ FGs made. That ties Adam Vinatieri for the most in a CAREER.** *

He went 14 for 14 on FGs during the postseason. That's the most FGs made in a single postseason in NFL history.

116. Cooper Kupp won the receiving triple crown, NFL Offensive Player of the Year, & Super Bowl MVP all in the 2021-22 season. *

Jerry Rice is the only other player to achieve all of these in a CAREER.

117. The team that loses the opening coin toss has won the last 8 Super Bowls. *

Super Bowl XLIX - Super Bowl LVI

118. Robbie Gould has NEVER missed a kick in the playoffs. *

21/21 on FGs, 34/34 on PATs

119. Jimmy Garoppolo has started in 3 playoff games where he didn't score a single TD passing or rushing. He's 3-0 in those games. *

Jimmy G's success in San Fran has been confusing. Interesting to see how that one plays out.

120.Since 2002, each team that has beaten the 49ers in the postseason won the Super Bowl that year. *

2002-03: Buccaneers
2011-12: Giants
2012-13: Ravens
2013-14: Seahawks
2019-20: Chiefs
2021-22: Rams

121.The QB who led the NFL in passing yards has NEVER won the Super Bowl that season. *

Eh no further comment from me on this one. Just keep enjoying the book!

122.In each of the last 5 years, the 6 seed has beaten the 3 seed in the NFC Wild Card Round. *

2017-18: (6) Falcons beat (3) Rams
2018-19: (6) Eagles beat (3) Bears
2019-20: (6) Vikings beat (3) Saints
2020-21: (6) Rams beat (3) Seahawks
2021-22: (6) 49ers beat (3) Cowboys

123.In Joe Burrow's first full NFL season, he led the Bengals to the Super Bowl. The last time the Bengals won a playoff game before that (1/6/1991), Joe Burrow wasn't even alive. *

Joe Burrow was born on 12/10/1996.

124.The Cowboys have gone 11 straight playoff appearances without reaching the conference championship game. *

That's the longest streak in NFL history by any team.

125.Ben Roethlisberger played 18 seasons in the NFL. He never was on a team that finished the season with a losing record. *

Not too shabby.

126.In his final career game at Heinz Field, Ben Roethlisberger became the first starting QB in NFL history to win a game with 40+ pass attempts & fewer than 150 passing yards. *

He was 24 of 46 for 123 yards 1 TD & 1 INT.

127. The Ravens have won 23 straight pre-season games dating back to 2016. *

Streak is still alive and it's an NFL record. 2nd most is 19 pre-season games by the Packers from 1959-1962.

128. The 2022 season is the 11th consecutive season that the Jaguars did not play on Monday Night Football. *

Jaguars not playing in prime time is a tradition. Check out the next stat.

129. The Jaguars are the only NFL team that's never played on Thanksgiving. *

And for that, I'm very thankful.

130.During the 2021-22 regular season, the Dolphins were 9-0 when the opposing starting QB's last name had an "o" in it & 0-8 when the opposing starting QB's last name didn't have an "o" in it. ⋆

Date	Opponent	Result	Score	Opposing QB
9/12/21	Patriots	WIN	17-16	Mac JOnes
9/19/21	Bills	LOSS	35-0	Josh Allen
9/26/21	Raiders	LOSS	31-28	Derek Carr
10/3/21	Colts	LOSS	27-17	Carson Wentz
10/10/21	Buccaneers	LOSS	45-17	Tom Brady
10/17/21	Jaguars	LOSS	23-20	Trevor Lawrence
10/24/21	Falcons	LOSS	30-28	Matt Ryan
10/31/21	Bills	LOSS	26-11	Josh Allen
11/7/21	Texans	WIN	17-9	Tyrod TaylOr
11/11/21	Ravens	WIN	22-10	Lamar JacksOn
11/21/21	Jets	WIN	24-17	Joe FlaccO
11/28/21	Panthers	WIN	33-10	Cam NewtOn
12/5/21	Giants	WIN	20-9	Mike GlennOn
12/19/21	Jets	WIN	31-24	Zach WilsOn

Date	Opponent	Result	Score	Opposing QB
12/27/21	Saints	WIN	20-3	Ian BOOk
1/2/22	Titans	LOSS	34-3	Ryan Tannehill
1/9/22	Patriots	WIN	33-24	Mac JOnes

131.Week 1 of 2022 was the first time since 2004 that the Browns won their first game of the season. *

To put that into perspective, 2004 was the year Facebook was launched.

132.In 2022, the Ravens became the first team in NFL history to hold a double-digit lead in each of their first 6 games & not have a winning record. *

How can they not finish these games with one of the best running QBs and the best kicker of all-time!?

133.September 18th, 2022 was the first time in over 10 years (12/11/11) that the Jets, Lions, & Jaguars won on the same day. *

9/18/22 was also the first time in almost 13 years (9/27/09) that the Mets, Yankees, Jets, & Giants all won on the same day.

134.On 10/10/2022, Travis Kelce became the first player in NFL history to have 4 receiving TDs of fewer than 10 yards each in a single game. *

He finished the game with 7 receptions for 25 yards & 4 TDs.

135.Patrick Mahomes has a better career winning percentage (59.1%, 13-9) when trailing by 10 or more points in a game than Kurt Warner's overall career winning percentage (58.9%). *

Mahomes is the only starting quarterback with a winning record when trailing by double digits in NFL history (minimum 10 games).

136.2022 was the first time in Jonathan Taylor's football career (including high school, college & NFL) where he missed a practice. *

We ain't even talking about a game, we talkin' bout practice!

137.Cooper Rush is the first QB since 1969 to have a game-winning drive in each of his first 3 career starts. *

Not bad for a backup.

138.On 11/13/2022, the Bears became the first team in NFL history to score at least 29 points in 3 consecutive games and lose all 3. *

Wow that historic Bears defense can't even keep teams under 30 points these days.

139.The Chargers are the only team to not have a player arrested in the last 5 years. *

Not bad for a team playing in LA.

140.From 2005-14, the Chargers only had 2 different kickers on their roster (Nate Kaeding '05-'11 & Nick Novak '11-'14). From 2017-2022, the Chargers have used 13 different kickers. *

At least now they have the kicker with the best nickname, "Dicker the Kicker"

141.There are only 2 quarterbacks in the Hall of Fame with the same middle name: John Constantine Unitas & Daniel Constantine Marino Jr. *

There's a fun trivia question for your buddies.

142.The Bills are the first team to win back-to-back games at Ford Field (Lion's stadium) since 2016. *

Pretty embarrassing for the Lions. Only reason the Bills did this is because one of their games got moved to Detroit due to weather in Buffalo then they played the Lions the next week.

143.2022 was the first time the New York Giants scored an offensive touchdown on Thanksgiving since 1938 vs. the Brooklyn Dodgers. *

They played 5 games on Thanksgiving during that span.

144.On 11/27/2022, the Jaguars won for the first time in franchise history when trailing by 7+ points in the final minute of regulation. They were 0-183 prior to that game. *

If it was any other team, this would be more surprising to me because 7 points doesn't seem like that big of a deficit.

145.The last 4 times the Saints have been shut out were all against the 49ers.

1997, 1998, 2002 & 2022

146. The Vikings have never lost on October 9th (Leif Erikson Day). *

Date	Opponent	Result	Score
10/9/65	Giants	WIN	40-14
10/9/77	Lions	WIN	14-7
10/9/83	Bears	WIN	23-14
10/9/88	Buccaneers	WIN	14-13
10/9/00	Buccaneers	WIN	30-23
10/9/11	Cardinals	WIN	34-10
10/9/16	Texans	WIN	31-13
10/9/17	Bears	WIN	20-17
10/9/22	Bears	WIN	29-22

147. This might be craziest one of them all. You need to see the video of these injuries too, almost identical.

Joe Theismann		Alex Smith
Washington Redskins	Team	Washington Redskins
Broken right tibia & fibula	Injury	Broken right tibia & fibula
Nov. 18th 1985	Date	Nov. 18th 2018
Washington D.C.	Location	Washington D.C.
23-21	Final Score	23-21
3-time DPOY Lawrence Taylor	Caused By	3-time DPOY J.J. Watt
Pro Bowl LT Joe Jacoby off field due to injury	Left Tackle	Pro Bowl LT Trent Williams off field due to injury

COLLEGE FOOTBALL STATS

148. On 10/7/1916, Georgia Tech beat Cumberland 222-0 in football.

Nothing to explain here, just your normal 222-0 blowout.

149. The 1939 matchup between Texas Tech & Centenary may be the weirdest college football game ever. They punted a total of 77 times!

13 NCAA records still stand from that game:

INDIVIDUAL
- **Most punts, game** - 36, Charlie Calhoun (Texas Tech)
- **Most punting yards, game** - 1,318, Charlie Calhoun (Texas Tech)
- **Most punt returns, game** - 20, Milton Hill (Texas Tech)
- **Most combined punt & kickoff returns, game** - 20 Milton Hill (Texas Tech)

TEAM
- **Most punts, both teams** - 77, Texas Tech & Centenary
- **Most punts, game** - 39, Texas Tech
- **Most punt returns, game** - 22 Texas Tech

- **Most punt returns, both teams** - 42 Texas Tech & Centenary
- **Fewest plays, game** - 12, Texas Tech
- **Fewest plays allowed, game** - 12, Centenary
- **Fewest plays, both team** - 33, Texas Tech & Centenary
- **Fewest rushes, both teams** - 28 Texas Tech & Centenary

Basically the weather was so bad, both teams decided to have a punt off, even on first down. This shootout ended 0-0.

150. Oklahoma won 47 straight games between 1953-1957. The longest win streak in D1 college football.

Don't know if this one will ever be broken.

151. Before passing, Dick Coffee attended 781 straight Alabama football games. The streak began in 1946 & ended at the 2013 BCS National Championship.

Mr. Coffee had to be included in this book for obvious reasons, but he doesn't even hold the record. Read the next stat.

152.Giles Pellerin holds the Guinness World Record for most consecutive games attended (797 straight USC football games).

His streak began in 1926 & ended in 1998 where he died in the Rose Bowl parking lot during the 2nd half of the USC-UCLA game.

153.As Virginia Tech's QB, Bruce Arians had more rushing TDs in a single season (11 in 1974) than Michael Vick did (9 in 1999 & 8 in 2000).

Therefore, Bruce Arians is a better runner than Michael Vick. Facts are facts.

154.Florida State and Florida played 13 times from 1990 to 2000. Both teams were ranked in the top 10 every single time. In 6 of those meetings, both teams were ranked in the top 5.

Looking at where these programs are now, this stat is even crazier.

155.In 2006, Florida won the football & basketball national championship.

No other school has won both in the same DECADE.

156.In 2010, 14 different players caught a pass for Auburn on their way to a 15-0 season. Cam Newton was the only one who also caught a pass in an NFL games.

It's stats like this that make you think Cam Newton was one of the greatest college QBs of all-time.

157.Just everything about Patrick Mahomes' & Baker Mayfield's performance in their 66-59 shootout in college.

MAHOMES		MAYFIELD
52-of-88	Passes	27-of-36
734	Yards	545
819	Total yards	564
5	Total TDs	7

158.When Patrick Mahomes (TTU) threw his first career TD pass, Tyreek Hill (Ok St.) also scored his first career TD in that same game.

Pretty crazy looking at where they are now. I doubt they even knew each other then.

159.As a sophomore, Lamar Jackson broke the Louisville school record for TDs in a game with 8. He did this in the FIRST HALF.

EIGHT! IN THE FIRST HALF!

160.Taysom Hill had 4 separate season-ending injuries in college.

3 of them were against Utah State.

10/5/2012	BYU vs. Utah State	Bicep femoris tendon detached from the bone
10/3/2014	BYU vs. Utah State	Broken fibula and shredded ligaments
9/5/2015	BYU vs. Nebraska	Lisfranc fracture
11/26/2016	BYU vs. Utah State	Hyper extended elbow causing tricep tendon to detach from bone

161. **There's been 24 College Football Playoff games so far. 75% (18/24) of those games have been won by either Alabama, Ohio State, or Clemson.**

Obviously this stat will change soon but too insane to not include it. Can't wait until the college playoff is extended.

162. **6'4", 350-lb guard Deonte Brown didn't allow a single sack in his 3 seasons at Alabama (865 snaps).**

3 seasons! 0 sacks! WTF!

163. **Since the end of his 1st season at Bama (2008), Nick Saban has more national championships (6) than losses at home (5).**

I mean this could change or they could win another national title before losing at home. Absolutely insane.

164. Every single recruit that Nick Saban has brought to Alabama & has played at least 3 seasons has won a National Championship.

No wonder they get the best recruits.

165. Only once since 2010 has Alabama been ranked outside of the top 2 in the AP preseason polls. They were #3 in 2015.

Nick Saban & Alabama should just have their own section in this book at this point.

166. From 1998-2022, Notre Dame is 0-8 in BCS & NY6 bowls. *

Only in their most recent NY6 bowl game (1/1/22) have they lost by less than 14 points.

167. Quarterbacks who played at Notre Dame have lost 24 straight starts in the NFL. *

4 by Brady Quinn
4 by Jimmy Clausen
15 by DeShone Kizer
1 by Ian Book

168.For the 2020 season, Oregon won the PAC-12 yet they didn't even win their division.

Gotta love how COVID creates these bizarre situations.

169.For the 2019 season, 1,380 rushing yards would be enough for 8th most among Power-5 RBs. Well that's how many yards Chubba Hubbard had AFTER contact that season.

The dude dominated. It may take reading that stat twice to understand the craziness.

170.Colorado has NEVER beaten USC. *

(0-16)

171. Since 2008, half (7/14) of the Heisman winners played at Oklahoma or Alabama.
Since 2015, 71% (5/7) of the Heisman winners played at Oklahoma or Alabama. *

2008 - Sam Bradford (OU)
2009 - Mark Ingram (BAMA)
2015 - Derrick Henry (BAMA)
2017 - Baker Mayfield (OU)
2018 - Kyler Murray (OU)
2020 - Devonta Smith (BAMA)
2021 - Bryce Young (BAMA)

172. Iowa has only had 2 head coaches since 1979.

Hayden Fry (1979-1998) & Kirk Ferentz (1999-present)

173. Jake Bentley was a starting D1 QB during 3 different presidential campaigns (2016-2021).

Thanks to medical redshirts & 2020 not counting towards eligibility for this to be possible.

174. During his 3 years at Cincinnati, (2019-21), Sauce Gardener allowed 0 TDs in coverage. *

He played over 1,000 career snaps in 33 career games.

175. Between 2011-2021 (11 seasons), North Dakota State has won 9 National Championships. *

May just be FCS but this is ridiculous. 2016 & 2020 were the only years they didn't win.

176. Middle Tennessee State is 3-0 all-time vs. Miami. *

That's the most wins without a loss by any team against Miami.

NBA STATS

177. Bill Russell & the Celtics won 8 straight NBA championships from 1959-1966.

8 straight!? Wtf

178. During a 13 year span (1957-1969), there were only 2 years the Boston Celtics didn't win the NBA title (1958 &1967).

As if the previous stat wasn't crazy enough

179. Magic Johnson finished top 3 in league MVP voting for 9 straight years.

1983: 3rd Place
1984: 3rd Place
1985: 2nd Place
1986: 3rd Place
1987: 1st Place
1988: 3rd Place
1989: 1st Place
1990: 1st Place
1991: 2nd Place

180.On 4/15/1984, John Lucas of the Rockets scored 0 points with 24 assists.

That's some unselfish basketball right there.

181.Eric Money played for 2 teams in the same game and scored for both the Nets & 76ers.

So the way this happened is they had to re-do the final quarter and a half due to some technical fouls getting out of control. By the time they replayed the game, Eric Money had been traded from the Nets to 76ers.

182.On 12/30/90, Scott Skiles had 30 assists in a game. No other player has done this.

No explanation needed here. I wonder if you're actually reading the little comments under each stat or skipping this part. I guess I'll never know.

183.During the 1990-91 season, the Sacramento Kings went 25-57. They were 24-17 at home & 1-40 on the road.

1-40!!!

184.During the 1992 Olympics, the Dream Team (U.S. Men's basketball team) never called a single timeout during the tournament.

If that doesn't show how dominate they were, idk what does.

185.During the 1993-94 season, Spud Webb (5'7") grabbed 313 rebounds. That's more than Klay Thompson (6'6") has ever had in a season.

The most rebounds Klay had in a season was 306. I wish stats could truly show how incredible it was for a 5'7" player to play at a high level in the NBA, but you'll need to watch highlights to truly appreciate it.

186.With the Spurs, Dennis Rodman went on a 3-game stretch where he had 77 rebounds & 0 points.

- 0 pts 25 reb
- 0 pts 24 reb
- 0 pts 28 reb

187. In 1998, Gary Trent was traded from the Blazers to the Raptors 41 games into his 3rd season.
In 2021, Gary Trent Jr. was traded from the Blazers to the Raptors 41 games into his 3rd season.

Yes, they're father and son.

188. A.C. Green played over 14 straight NBA seasons (1,192 consecutive games) without missing a single game.

Idk what's crazier, this stat or the fact that he was a virgin until he was 38.

189. Tyrone "Muggsy" Bogues is the shortest player in NBA history (5'3") yet he still had 39 career blocks.

You thought Spud Webb at 5'7" was impressive, just playing in the NBA at 5'3" is a WTF Stat. Now who the heck was getting blocked by Muggsy!?

190. On 12/9/04, Tracy McGrady scored 13 points in the final 33 seconds of a comeback win.

If you haven't seen this, stop what you're doing right now and go watch this on youtube.

191.On 1/6/2005, Richard Hamilton become the only player in NBA history to lead his team in scoring in a game where he didn't make any FGs.

He went 0 for 10 on FGs but 14 for 14 on free throws.

192.Ben Wallace had more career steals than turnovers & more career blocks than fouls. He's the only NBA player to do either.

Read that 2 more times. He's the only player to do either of those!

1,369 steals   1,061 turnovers
2,137 blocks   2078 fouls

193.Chauncey Billups is the only player in NBA history to have a winning record vs. Michael Jordan, Kobe Bryant & LeBron James.

That Pistons team was something else.

194.Steve Kerr has won 12% of all NBA championships. *

5 as a player 4 as a coach

195.Phil Jackson has won 17% of all NBA championships. *

2 as a player, 11 as a coach

196.The Lakers & Celtics have won 45% (34/76) of all NBA Championships. *

And people are complaining about super teams now and how they dominate the league. The NBA has always been dominated by familiar faces.

197.Only 76 players in NBA history have ATTEMPTED more free throws than Shaq has MISSED (5,317).

Really read that again. More than he's MISSED!

198.During his NBA career, Shaquille O'Neal had more broken backboards (2) than made threes (1).

That's just too many broken backboards & not enough threes.

199.In the 2003-04 season, Carmelo Anthony won rookie of the month every single month of the season but didn't win rookie of the year.

So he won Rookie of the Month in the Western Conference every month while LeBron won it every month for the Eastern Conference & LeBron won Rookie of the Year.

200.In 2007, Kobe Bryant went on a crazy scoring stretch where he scored 50+ points in 7 out of 16 games & averaged 41 points per game over 30 days:

3/16/07: 65 pts vs. Trailblazers
3/18/07: 50 pts vs. Timberwolves
3/22/07: 60 pts vs. Grizzlies
3/23/07: 50 pts vs. Hornets
3/25/07: 43 pts vs. Warriors
3/27/07: 23 pts vs. Grizzlies
3/30/07: 53 pts vs. Rockets
4/01/07: 19 pts vs. Kings
4/03/07: 39 pts vs. Nuggets
4/04/07: 29 pts vs. Clippers
4/06/07: 46 pts vs. SuperSonics
4/08/07: 34 pts vs. Suns
4/09/07: 23 pts vs. Nuggets
4/12/07: 50 pts vs. Clippers
4/13/07: 17 pts vs. Suns
4/15/07: 50 pts vs. SuperSonics

201. Kobe Bryant never won an NBA championship without Derek Fisher.

And vis versa. Kinda weird for a 5-time NBA Champion.

202. In July of 2015, former 1st round pick Luke Ridnour was traded 4 times in less than a week.

Magic - (Wed. 7/24) -> Grizzlies (Thurs. 7/25) -> Hornets (Thurs. 7/25, hours later) -> Thunder (Tues.7/30) -> Raptors

203. In the 2015-16 season, all 3 point guards for the Mavericks were all born on the same day (6/26/84).

Deron Williams, Raymond Felton, J.J. Barea

204. When Steph Curry was the unanimous MVP in 2016, he also finished 4th in the voting for the Most Improved Player. He won MVP the previous season.

Just read that again.

205.On 2/10/2017, Draymond Green got a triple-double while only scoring 4 points.

10 assists, 10 steals, 12 rebounds, 4 points, 5 blocks

206.On 2/24/2017 vs. the Jazz, Tony Snell (MIL) played 28 minutes and put up 0 points, 0 rebounds, 0 assists, 0 blocks & 0 steals.

Bonus stat: This same player is the first player in NBA history to have a 50/50/100 season.
50.9 FG%   56.9 3P%   100 FT%

Double Bonus stat: he also hasn't missed a free throw since 3/12/2019. During the last 3 seasons (2019-2022), he's shot 100% on free throws (47/47). *

207.In a game on 1/8/19, Klay Thompson scored 43 points on only 4 dribbles.

Wish I could show you how the highlights of this but if you try that ol internet thing, you could probably find it.

208.During the 2018 season, 6'11" Nikola Jokić had more triple-doubles (12) than dunks (11).

This stat makes no sense to me.

209.Devin Booker never started a single game in college.

He was still 3rd on the team in scoring.

210.The 1971-72 & 2019-20 NBA seasons were very, VERY similar.

1971-72	2019-20
Wilt Chamberlain (LAL) 34 years old, turned 35 during season	LeBron James (LAL) 34 years old, turned 35 during season
Kareem Abdul-Jabbar (MIL) - 24 years old, turned 25 during season	Giannis Antetokounmpo (MIL) - 24 years old, turned 25 during season
Lakers & Bucks both top 3 regular season records	Lakers & Bucks both top 3 regular season records
Wilt Chamberlain (LAL) had 4 MVPs entering the season	LeBron James (LAL) had 4 MVPs entering the season
Kareem Abdul-Jabbar (MIL) won his 2nd MVP	Giannis Antetokounmpo (MIL) won his 2nd MVP
Wilt Chamberlain & Lakers won championship	LeBron James & Lakers won championship

211.2021 was the first time in franchise history (since 1967) that the Spurs failed to make the playoffs in back-to-back seasons.

Absolutely absurd. Granted, over half the league makes the playoffs which is also absurd.

212.The year Kobe passed, this happened:

Kobe Bryant in 2009 Playoffs	LeBron James in 2020 Playoffs
Beat Rockets in 2nd round	Beat Rockets in 2nd round
Beat Nuggets in WCF	Beat Nuggets in WCF
Won his 4th ring in Orlando	Won his 4th ring in Orlando

213.Chris Paul has blown a 2-0 lead in a 7-game series 5 different times. *Most in NBA history.* *

Still a great player but damn, that's gotta sting.

214.Every NBA Finals from 1984-2020 included at least one player who was a teammate of Shaq's.

Finals year	Finals matchup	Most notable teammate	Years played with Shaq
1984	Celtics vs. Lakers	Greg Kite (Boston Celtics)	Orlando Magic (1992-94)
1985	Lakers vs. Celtics	Byron Scott (Los Angeles Lakers)	Lakers (1996-97)
1986	Celtics vs. Rockets	Greg Kite (Boston Celtics)	Orlando Magic (1992-94)
1987	Lakers vs. Celtics	A.C. Green (Los Angeles Lakers)	Lakers (1999-2000)
1988	Lakers vs. Pistons	A.C. Green (Los Angeles Lakers)	Lakers (1999-2000)
1989	Pistons vs. Lakers	Dennis Rodman (Detroit Pistons)	Lakers (1999)
1990	Pistons vs. Trail Blazers	John Salley (Detroit Pistons)	Lakers (1999-2000)
1991	Bulls vs. Lakers	Horace Grant (Chicago Bulls)	Magic (1994-96); Lakers (2000-01; 03-04)
1992	Bulls vs. Trail Blazers	Horace Grant (Chicago Bulls)	Magic (1994-96); Lakers (2000-01; 03-04)

1993	Bulls vs. Suns	Horace Grant (Chicago Bulls)	Magic (1994-96); Lakers (2000-01; 03-04)
1994	Rockets vs. Knicks	Robert Horry (Houston Rockets)	Lakers (1996-03)
1995	Rockets vs. Magic	Robert Horry (Houston Rockets)	Lakers (1996-03)
1996	Bulls vs. SuperSonics	Steve Kerr (Chicago Bulls)	Magic (1992-93)
1997	Bulls vs. Jazz	Ron Harper (Chicago Bulls)	Lakers (1999-01)
1998	Bulls vs. Jazz	Ron Harper (Chicago Bulls)	Lakers (1999-01)
1999	Spurs vs. Knicks	Jerome Kersey (San Antonio Spurs)	Lakers (1996-97)
2000	Lakers vs. Pacers	All Lakers	
2001	Lakers vs. 76ers	All Lakers	
2002	Lakers vs. Nets	All Lakers	
2003	Spurs vs. Nets	Steve Kerr (San Antonio Spurs)	Magic (1992-93)
2004	Pistons vs. Lakers	Elden Campbell (Detroit Pistons)	Lakers (1996-99)

2005	Spurs vs. Pistons	Robert Horry (San Antonio Spurs)	Lakers (1996-03)
2006	Heat vs. Mavericks	All Heat players	
2007	Spurs vs. Cavaliers	Robert Horry (San Antonio Spurs)	Lakers (1996-03)
2008	Celtics vs. Lakers	Paul Pierce (Boston Celtics)	Celtics (2010-11)
2009	Lakers vs. Magic	Kobe Bryant (Los Angeles Lakers)	Lakers (1996-04)
2010	Lakers vs. Celtics	Kobe Bryant (Los Angeles Lakers)	Lakers (1996-04)
2011	Mavericks vs. Heat	LeBron James (Miami Heat)	Cavaliers (2009-10)
2012	Heat vs. Thunder	Udonis Haslem (Miami Heat)	Heat (2004-08)
2013	Heat vs. Spurs	Ray Allen (Miami Heat)	Celtics (2010-11)
2014	Spurs vs. Heat	Danny Green (San Antonio Spurs)	Cavaliers (2009-10)
2015	Warriors vs. Cavaliers	Leandro Barbosa (Golden State Warriors)	Suns (2008-09)

2016	Cavaliers vs. Warriors	Mo Williams (Cleveland Cavaliers)	Cavaliers (2009-10)
2017	Warriors vs. Cavaliers	Matt Barnes (Golden State Warriors)	Suns (2008-09)
2018	Warriors vs. Cavaliers	LeBron James (Cleveland Cavaliers)	Cavaliers (2009-10)
2019	Raptors vs. Warriors	Danny Green (Toronto Raptors)	Cavaliers (2009-10)
2020	Lakers vs. Heat	LeBron James (Los Angeles Lakers)	Cavaliers (2009-10)

215. Brook Lopez made 3 3-pointers during his first 8 seasons in the NBA (.097 3P%).
In his next 5 seasons, he made 630 3-pointers (.344 3P%)

Great stat to show how much the game has changed, even for the big guys.

216. Kawhi Leonard has more Finals MVPs (2) than triple-doubles (1) in his NBA career.

One of a kind stat for a one of a kind guy.

217. Steph Curry has a career high of 62 points in a regular season game. Sounds impressive but a Warriors player has scored 62+ points in a game 21 other times.

Thanks to a 64-point game by Rick Barry, a 63-point game by Joe Fulks & 19 games by Wilt Chamberlain where he scored at least 62 for the Warriors.

218. Boban Marjanović is 7'4" but his parents are 5'6" & 5'9".

WTF

219. In the 2020-21 season, Draymond Green became the first player in NBA history to finish the regular season with more assists (558) than points (444) AND more rebounds (449) than points.

Like he said himself, why would he shoot the ball when he's got Steph as a teammate.

220.In 2021, Chris Paul became the first player with 15 points, 15 assists, & 0 turnovers in a playoff game since... Chris Paul in 2014 who was the first player to do so since... Chris Paul in 2008.

See here's a good stat to show how great CP3 really is in the postseason.

221.During the 2021 postseason, Ben Simmons finished with the worst free throw shooting percentage in NBA playoffs history (34.2%). He's a point guard.

I know you knew this one but this is so embarrassingly bad. Don't forget he was drafted #1 overall.

222. Steph Curry has more career regular season games with 10+ 3-pointers made than the next 10 people on that list combined.

Steph Curry: 22
Klay Thompson: 5
James Harden: 3
Damian Lillard: 3
JR Smith: 3
Zach LaVine: 2
19 other players: 1

223.Tim Duncan has more career wins (1,158) than the Minnesota Timberwolves (1,079). Tim Duncan played 19 seasons in the NBA while the Timberwolves have been in the NBA for 33 seasons.

This includes playoffs. I know this stat will change eventually but this has gone on for way too long!

224.The Grizzlies are the only NBA franchise that haven't had a player score 50 or more points in a game.

Alright Ja Morant, your move. He scored 49 points on 10/21/2022.

225.Rasheed Wallace has twice as many ejections (29) as any other player in NBA history.

Demarcus Cousins is next highest with 14.

226.Dwight Howard missed more free throws (366) during the 2012-13 season than Steve Nash missed during his entire 18-year NBA career (324).

Dwight Howard went 355/721 (49.2%) in 2012-12.

Steve Nash went 3,060/3,384 (90.4%) in his NBA career.

227.Both Lonzo & his brother LaMelo Ball broke the NBA record for the youngest player to score a triple-double.

Lonzo 11/11/2017
LaMelo 1/9/2021

228.On 3/3/21, T.J. McConnell set the NBA record for most steals in a half with 9.

McConnell finished the game with 10.
The record for most steals in a game is 11.

229.In NBA history, a team has never finished a game with 0 turnovers. Only once has a team finished a game with 1 turnover. (Nuggets 2/23/21)

So close but no cigar.

230.There's been 74 Eastern Conference Finals. The Celtics have played in exactly half of them (37). *

Obviously this will change soon but wtf!

231.The most recent Western Conference team not from California or Texas to win an NBA championship is the 1979 Seattle Supersonics.

The Suns almost broke this streak, but they didn't.

232.Among players with at least 2,500 attempts, Russell Westbrook has the worst 3-point percentage in NBA history (30.5%).

Among players with 2,000 attempts, Charles Barkley has the worst 3P% (26.6%).

233. Every single NBA Finals (76 years) has featured at least 1 player who played for the Knicks at some point in their career. *

2022 Luke Kornet (BOS)
2021 Bobby Portis (MIL)
2020 J.R. Smith (LAL)
2019 Jeremy Lin (TOR)
2018 JR Smith (CLE)
2017 JR Smith (CLE)
2017 Matt Barnes (GSW)
2016 Channing Frye (CLE)
2015 David Lee (GSW)
2014 Toney Douglas (MIA)
2013 Tracy McGrady (SAS)
2012 Eddy Curry (MIA)
2011 Tyson Chandler (DAL)
2010 Nate Robinson (BOS)
2009 Trevor Ariza (LAL)
2008 Eddie House (BOS)
2007 Jackie Butler (SAS)
2006 Michael Doleac (MIA)
2005 Nazr Mohammad (SAS)
2004 Rasheed Wallace (DET)
2003 Malik Rose (SAS)
2002 Jason Kidd (NJN)
2001 Dikembe Mutombo (PHI)
2000 Glen Rice (LAL)
1999 Charlie Ward (NYK)
1998 Shandon Anderson (UTA)
1997 Howard Eisley (UTA)
1996 Luc Longley (CHI)

1995 Penny Hardaway (ORL)
1994 Herb Williams (NYK)
1993 Trent Tucker (CHI)
1992 Buck Williams (POR)
1991 Bill Cartwright (CHI)
1990 Buck Williams (POR)
1989 Tony Campbell (LAL)
1988 Tony Campbell (LAL)
1987 Rick Carlisle (BOS)
1986 Rick Carlisle (BOS)
1985 Rick Carlisle (BOS)
1984 Greg Kite (BOS)
1983 Maurice Cheeks (PHI)
1982 Maurice Cheeks (PHI)
1981 Gerald Henderson (BOS)
1980 Maurice Cheeks (PHI)
1979 Lonnie Shelton (SEA)
1978 Marvin Webster (SEA)
1977 Henry Bibby (PHI)
1976 Dick Van Arsdale (PHX)
1975 Butch Beard (GSW)
1974 Dick Garrett (MIL)
1973 Willis Reed (NYK)
1972 Dave DeBusschere (NYK)
1971 Earl Monroe (BAL)
1970 Walt Frazier (NYK)
1969 Jim Barnes (BOS)
1968 Jim Barnes (LAL)
1967 Art Heyman (PHI)
1966 Willie Naulls (BOS)
1965 Willie Naulls (BOS)
1964 Wilie Naulls (BOS)
1963 Dick Barnett (LAL)
1962 Carl Braun (BOS)

1961 Gene Conley (BOS)
1960 Slater Martin (STL)
1959 Gene Conley (BOS)
1958 Slater Martin (STL)
1957 Slater Martin (STL)
1956 Tom Gola (PHW)
1955 Connie Simmons (SYR)
1954 Slater Martin (SNL)
1953 Dick McGuire (NYK)
1952 Nat Clifton (NYK)
1951 Harry Gallatin (NYK)
1950 Slater Martin (MNL)
1949 Sonny Hertzberg (WSC)

234. Michael Jordan & LeBron James both won their 4th championship & 4th Finals MVP the season after filming Space Jam.

Who doesn't love a good MJ/LJ comparison?

235. The NBA MVP has averaged less than 20 PPG since 1981 only twice.

Both times were Steve Nash.

2004-05 15.5 PPG
2005-06 18.8 PPG

236. In the history of the NBA, there's only been 4 players named T.J. All 4 played for the Pacers. 3 of them at the same time (2020).

Who finds these ridiculous stats!? Oh wait... I do.

237. Vince Carter is the only NBA player to play in 4 different decades. (1990's, 2000's, 2010's, 2020's)

Just perfect timing for this. He played 22 seasons from 1999-2020.

238. The Spurs are the only NBA franchise that are at least .500 against all other 29 teams. *

As of now (11/29/22), the Spurs are 92-92 vs. the Lakers all time.

239. 16-year veteran Mike Conley has never received a technical foul. Ever. Not in high school, not in college, not in the NBA. *

He did get charged one in 2015 but the call would later be rescinded.

240.Since 1982, Melbourne, Australia has been the birth place to more #1 overall picks than any other city in the world.

2017: Ben Simmons
2011: Kyrie Irving
2005: Andrew Bogut
Chicago & Toronto both have 2.

241.LeBron James has more followers on Instagram (138M) than the NFL, NBA, MLB, & NHL COMBINED. *

NBA: 73M   NFL: 25.9M   MLB: 9.3M   NHL: 5.7M

242.LeBron James reached the NBA Finals for 8 STRAIGHT YEARS (2011-2018). *

I feel like everyone knows this stat but it's still pretty ridiculous. 5 other players have done this but they all played for the Celtics in the 60's.

243.Luka Dončić faced as many ALL-NBA 1st/2nd team players in 3 playoff runs as LeBron James did during his 8-straight Finals runs in the Eastern Conference. *

Not to take anything away from LeBron, but this stat just shows how much better the Western Conference has been in recent years than the Eastern Conference.

244.On 2/2/22, #22 Desmond Bane recorded this stat line: *

22.2 FG% 2 AST 2 STL 2 BLK 2 TO 2 PF

Oh yeah and his birthday was 222 days before this game.

245.The Denver Nuggets' mascot's salary is over twice as much ($625,000) as the HIGHEST salary in the WNBA (Jewell Loyd: $228,094). *

To be fair, more people watch the Nuggets mascot than the WNBA.

COLLEGE BASKETBALL STATS

246. **James Naismith, the man who invented basketball, is the only head coach in Kansas men's basketball history with a losing record.**

He lost more often than he won at his own game!

247. **From 1967-73, UCLA won 7 straight NCAA men's basketball championships.**

This will never happen again. I guarantee it.

248. **From 1964-1975, there were only 2 seasons where UCLA didn't win the NCAA basketball championship.**

Just when you thought the previous stat couldn't get any crazier…BOOM!

249. On 1/12/92, Troy State beat DeVry 258-141. Highest scoring game in NCAA history.

How does this even happen!? That's an average of a point scored every 6 seconds.

250. 234 different D1 teams have won an NCAA Tournament game. Nebraska still hasn't.

It's not like they're a new program. They've been playing since 1896 & have made 7 NCAA Tournament appearances.

251. Temple has made 33 appearances in the NCAA Tournament.
They're 33-33 in NCAA Tournament games.

Confusing I know. But it makes sense, just think about it.

252. On 11/20/2012, Jack Taylor scored 138 points in an NCAA basketball game.

138 points is an absurd amount for a team! They (Grinnell College) won 179-104.

Jack Taylor's stats were:
52/108 FG
27/71 3PT
7/10 FT
138 PTS

Nobody else on his team scored more than 13 points. On the losing team (Faith Baptist Bible), David Larsen had quite the game too.

David Larsen's stats:
34/44 FG
0/2 3PT
2/4 FT
70 PTS

Nobody else on his team scored more than 8 points.

253. During the 2020-21 season, Gonzaga won 22 straight games by double digits. First NCAAM team to do this since UCLA in 1968-69.

Now you know it's a crazy stat is we're comparing it to the old UCLA days.

254.2021 was the first UNC-Duke men's basketball game where both teams were unranked since 1960.

That's over 60 years and they place twice a year. I'll let you do the rest of the math.

255.2021 was also the first time since 1961 where Duke, North Carolina & Kentucky were all not in the men's AP Top 25 at the same time.

Again, 60 years…

256.As North Carolina's head coach, Roy Williams had a career record of 485-163 (74.8%) but against Texas, he was only 1-8 (11.1%).

If you know anything about college basketball, you know how bizarre this is.

257.There's been 67 ACC Men's basketball championship games. Only once has the game not featured a team from North Carolina.

1990: Georgia Tech vs Virginia

258. On 1/18/20, Vanderbilt went 0/25 from 3-point range.

Thankfully nobody keeps stats of me shooting around at the gym, but if they did, I still think I've never been THIS bad.

MLB STATS

259.In the 1886 World Series, there were a total of 54 errors made.

I've seen tee-ball teams go an entire season with less errors than this.

260.During the 1879 season, Reds pitcher Will White pitched 75 complete games.

The Reds only played 81 games that season.

261.In 1893, a baseball game ended with a final score of 2.5-2 because a player broke his bat, picked up an axe, and hit half the ball over the fence.

Tough to verify this but I did see it in a newspaper article from 1893. What a wild time.

262.In 1909, Ty Cobb led MLB with 9 HRs. They were all inside the park.

Ty Cobb finished his career with 46 inside the park HRs. 4th all-time.

263.In 1917, Ernie Shore threw 27 straight outs without allowing a baserunner. He didn't get a perfect game because he didn't start the game.

Babe Ruth started the game, walked the first batter and then got ejected for punching the umpire.

264.In 1919, Ray Caldwell pitched a complete game despite being struck by lightning in the 9th inning.

They just don't make 'em like they used to. This stat was runner-up in the WTF Madness.

265.From 1918-1948, the Phillies only had 1 winning season. 78-76 in 1932.

Translation: The Phillies were not good at baseball for 30 years yet they continued to keep playing.

266.On 8/17/1957, a lady got hit with 2 foul balls in the same at-bat.

Just imagine how great this would be in the social media days, assuming she's ok of course.

267.Hall of Fame pitcher Hoyt Williams hit a HR in his first career at-bat, then a triple in his 2nd at-bat. That would be his only HR and his only triple of his 20+ year career.

Yeah, go ahead and read that one again to get a full grasp of how crazy that is.

268.In his 23 years in the MLB, Hank Aaron had 25 all-star appearances (MLB Record).

As much as I don't want to explain this one & leave you confused, I will. They used to have 2 all-star games per season.

269.If you changed all of Ted Williams' 521 HRs to strikeouts, he'd still have a higher OBP than Hank Aaron.

OBP = On Base Percentage
Ted Williams' OBP: .482
Hank Aaron's OBP: .374
Ted Williams' OBP w/o HRs: .428

270.In 1968 from June-August, Bob Gibson started 18 games and pitched 9 innings 17 times.

He pitched 11 innings the other time.

271.Warren Spahn had 363 career wins and 363 career hits. He had 356 wins and 356 hits with the Braves, 4 wins and 4 hits with the Mets and 3 wins and 3 hits with the Giants. He also had 4 postseason wins and 4 postseason hits.

Oh don't believe me? Then wtf you doing reading this book? It's true.

272.Stan Musial had 3,630 career hits. 1,815 at home and 1,815 on the road.

Aren't these type of stats just so satisfying?

273.Ken Griffey Jr. has 2,781 career hits in his 22-year MLB career. That's not even the most for players born in Donora, Pennsylvania on November 21st. That record would belong to Stan Musial (3,630 career hits) who was also born in Donora, Pennsylvania on November 21st.

Want your son to be in the Baseball Hall of Fame? I think you know where to go on delivery day.
Hint: February 21st is 9 months before November 21st.

274. On 6/12/1970, Dock Ellis threw a no-hitter while under the influence of LSD.

Ellis D. Get it? Like LSD, Ellis D.

275. On 6/14/1974, Nolan Ryan threw 235 pitches in a game.

It's rare these days for a pitcher to throw 100 pitches.

276. On 7/29/1989, Rickey Henderson recorded this stat line: *

0/0	4 R	4 BB	5 SB

They just don't make em like they used to. Don't think we'll see anything like this again.

277. Tony Cloninger holds the Braves franchise record for most RBIs in a game with 9. He was a pitcher.

He only hit 9+ RBIs in a SEASON once during his 12 year career. He hit 23 in 1966.

278.**Only 2 players in MLB history have hit 5 HRs in a double header: Stan Musial & Nate Colbert.**

As a kid, Nate Colbert attended the games where Musial hit 5 HRs.

279.**Even if you removed Hank Aaron's 755 career HRs, he would still be 1 of only 33 MLB players with 3,000 career hits.** *

R.I.P. Hank

280.**During his MLB career, Nolan Ryan struck out 8 different father/son combos.**

Like the Tom Brady of baseball

281.**Nolan Ryan has 5,714 career strikeouts. Nobody else has over 5,000. Only 3 other players have over 4,000.**

Greatest pitcher ever. Not up for debate.

282.If an MLB player had 60 stolen bases a season for 23 straight years, he still wouldn't break Rickey Henderson's career stolen base record (1,406).

To put that in perspective, no player has stolen more than 50 bases in any of the last 4 seasons.

283.Tommy John's career was so long (26 seasons), that he's the only pitcher to face Mickey Mantel & Mark McGwire.

This sounds so crazy that it sounds made up, but it's true. And yes, the surgery was named after him.

284.During the 1994 season that was shortened by the strike, the Padres won 47 games. Tony Gwynn played in 45 of those games and batted .511.

Oh you want some more crazy Tony Gwynn stats? I got you

285.Tony Gwynn has more 4-hit games (45) than 2-strikeout (34) games in his MLB career.

Translation: He got a lot of hits but didn't strike out much.

286.Tony Gwynn stats vs. these great pitchers:

Greg Maddux
107 PA, .415 BA, 0 K

Tom Glavine
105 PA, .303 BA, 2 K

John Smoltz
75 PA, .444 BA, 1 K

Curt Schilling
43 PA, .390 BA, 2 K

Pedro Martinez
36 PA, .314 BA, 0 K

287.On 7/22/1997, Greg Maddux threw a complete game using just 77 pitches.

Only 14 were balls.

288.If Greg Maddux threw a complete game in every one of his career starts (740), he'd still have fewer complete games than Cy Young (749).

Cy Young pitched a complete game in 92% (749/815) of his starts.

289. Mark McGwire's record-setting 70 HRs in the '98 season traveled a total of 29,598 feet. Enough to fly over Mount Everest.

To be honest, probably my least favorite stat in this book. Feels like a weird comparison but seems to be a fan favorite so here you go.

290. On 4/23/99, Fernando Tatis Sr. hit 2 grand slams in the same inning.

The same inning!!! Idk if anyone will even have the opportunity to do this ever again.

291. Cal Ripken Jr. played in 2,632 consecutive MLB games. That's over 16 seasons without missing a game.

Just playing 16 seasons is impressive.

292. During his entire 4-year high school career, Joe Mauer only struck out once.

I know it's high school but damn! That pitcher has bragging rights for life.

293.More men have walked on the moon (12) than have scored an earned run against Mariano Rivera in the postseason (11).

Love everything about this stat. Both are amazing feats.

294.Since 1960, nobody has been over .500 in on-base percentage except Barry Bonds, who's done it 3 times.

He had an OBP of .609 in 2004

295.On 7/1/1990, Andy Hawkins threw a no-hitter & lost.

5 walks and 3 errors by the defense led to a 4-0 loss.

296.Ken Griffey & and his son Ken Griffey Jr. not only played on the same MLB team, but they hit back-to-back HRs in a game!

Just insane. What dreams are made of.

297. Ken Griffey Jr. hit his 400th HR on his dad's 50th birthday & his 500th HR on Father's Day.

Again, what dreams are made of.

298. In June of 1998, Sammy Sosa hit 20 HRs. He averaged a HR every 5.7 at-bats that month.

What!? Every 5.7 at-bats!?

299. The Mariners hold the MLB record for the most wins in a season with 116 yet they're the only MLB team that's never been to a World Series.

Incredible stat but also incredibly sad.

300. Only 7 times in MLB history has a player hit over 60 HRs in a season. Sammy Sosa has done it 3 times.

Damn I miss those days where juiced players were going yard 60-70 times a year.

301. On 5/12/2001, A.J. Burnett threw a no-hitter where he allowed each starting position player to reach base safely.

This is just such a weird stat. I hope you love weird stats as much as me because I've been going over each stat like 5-10 times and they still blow my mind.

302. On 5/23/2002, Shawn Green went 6 for 6 with 4 HRs & 19 total bases. *

19 total bases is still an MLB record. 18 players have hit 4 HRs in a game but no one has ever hit 5.

303. In 2004, Barry Bonds had 373 at-bats but reached base safely 376 times.

He also turned 40 that season.

304. In 2008, CC Sabathia led both the NL & AL in shutouts.

He got traded that season from the Indians to the Brewers.

305. On 4/13/2009, Jermaine Dye & Paul Konerko each hit their 300th career HR on back-to-back at-bats.

If you go watch this video on youtube, you'll be amazed at how little of a reaction you get from the announcers.

306. On 4/18/2012, Bartolo Colon threw 38 consecutive strikes.

Most since 1988.

307. If 3-time Cy Young winner Clayton Kershaw were to break Cy Young's record of 511 wins, he'd need to stay at his current pace (13.1 wins a year) for the next 25 years. He'd be 58.

Ok maybe Cy Young is the best pitcher of all-time.

308. Khris Davis's batting average:
2015: .247   2016: .247
2017: .247   2018: .247

Mr. consistent. I'm sure he wishes that average was a little higher. His career average is .242.

309. On Mother's Day in 2016, Bryce Harper reached base 7 different times but didn't have a single at-bat.

Yep sounds as weird as it is. He was walked 6 times. He saw 27 pitches & only 2 of them were strikes.

310. In 2016, Clayton Kershaw had more wins (12) than walks (11).

Absolutely unreal. Not sure how often this happens.

311. Both Prince Fielder & his father Cecil Fielder finished their MLB career with exactly 319 home runs.

Like father, like son.

312. Madison Bumgarner has never allowed a run in a winner-take-all playoff game. (23 total innings)

If you look up clutch in the dictionary, this stat might just be there.

313. On 8/25/2019, the Mets tied the MLB record by striking out 26 batters in a game. They still lost.

Glad to see a good stat Mets fans can hang their hat on.

314. Joey Gallo had 100 career HRs before 100 career singles.

You know this actually makes sense because it's easier to hit a HR than just a base hit. Everyone knows that.

315. Ichiro's 1st MLB game (2001): Mariners beat A's 5-4 Ichrio's last MLB game (2019): Mariners beat A's 5-4

It's not about how you start, it's how you finish. Which in this case, is the exact same.

316. Before recording his first hit of his MLB career, Patrick Mazeika had 2 walk-off RBI's.

What a bizarre start to his MLB career in 2021. Both were fielder's choice ground balls where they threw to home and didn't get the runner.

317. **On 8/19/20, starting pitchers Casey Mize & Dane Dunning had very similar stats when they faced off in their MLB debut.**

Casey Mize	Round Drafted	Dane Dunning
1st	Round Drafted	1st
8/19/20 vs. White Sox	Debut	8/19/20 vs. Tigers
4 1/3	Innings Pitched	4 1/3
3	Earned Runs	3
6.23	ERA	6.23
73	Pitches Thrown	73

318. **On 5/2/2019, Noah Syndergaard pitched a complete game shutout where they won 1-0. The only run came from the HR he hit.**

I hope he was player of the game.

319. Kyle Seager has been a part of 9 no-hitters.

Played Against:
Philip Humber (2012)
Angels combined (2019)
Astros combined (2019)
John Means (2021)
Spencer Turnbull (2021)

Played For:
Félix Hernández (2012)
Mariners combined (2012)
Hisashi Iwakuma (2015)
James Paxton (2018)

320. During the 2021 season, Jacob deGrom became the first pitcher in MLB history to have more RBIs (5) than ER (4) over any 10-start span in a single season since the RBI become an official stat (1920).

I love how we're just seeing some really good hitting pitchers and then we make a universal DH rule.

321. Both Daz Cameron & his father Mike Cameron have stolen a base off Yadier Molina.

I can't tell if this stat is impressive for Yadier or not.

322.258 games into his MLB career, Vladimir Guerrero had 50 HRs. 258 games into his MLB career, Vladimir Guerrero Jr. had 50 HRs.

Starting to see a lot of father-son stats in this book.

323.On 7/11/21, Marlins pitcher Pablo Lopez struck out the first 9 batters of the game. First player to do this since 1884.

This was also the Braves first game without Ronald Acuña Jr. after he tore his ACL. Somehow the Braves still won the World Series.

324.In 2012, the Oakland A's drafted Max Muncy who was born on August 25th. In 2021, the Oakland A's drafted Max Muncy who was born on August 25th.

Yep nothing to explain here.

325.For the 2021 MLB Draft, the Angels had 20 picks. They picked 20 pitchers.

Maybe they'll find 1 or 2 so they can actually get to the playoffs.

326. **On 7/28/2021, during the Twins-Tigers game, the Twins hit 7 HRs while the Tigers hit 0 HRs. The Twins still lost 14-17.**

Pretty crazy game. The Twins were down 10-0 in the 4th.

327. **On 7/26/2021, Abraham Toro homered for the Astros against the Mariners. On 7/27/2021, Abraham Toro homered for the Mariners against the Astors.**

Had to be weird to get traded mid-series to the other team.

328. **Rodolfo Castro's first 5 hits of his MLB career were all HRs.**

68 at-bats later, and he hasn't hit a HR since his 5th.

329. **Saby Zavala hit his first 3 career HRs all in the same game. Only player in MLB history to do this.**

Not sure which stat is more impressive, this one or the previous one. I think this one.

330. **During his 11-year MLB career, Wade Miley has been the starting pitcher at Citi Field (Mets' Stadium) 4 times. All 4 times, he got a no-decision & the final score was 5-4.**

Just so specific & so weird.

331. **On 8/6/2021, Will Matthiessen (OF for Pirates single-A team) pitched for the first time in his pro career. He gave up 6 runs in the top of the 12th, but then hit a walk-off grand slam in the bottom of the 12th.**

What a roller coaster of emotions for that guy.

332. **On 8/10/21, Miguel Sánchez got his first career win as a pitcher in the big leagues. He only threw 1 pitch & it resulted in a strikeout.**

Now that's efficient.

333. **Nick Markakis had more hits (2,388) during his MLB career than swing & misses (1,969).**

So if he swings the bat, there's better chance of it being a hit than him missing the ball… wtf

334. Cardinals' Stephen Piscotty got hit by the ball 3 times in 1 inning.

He got hit by a pitch, then got hit by a throw sliding into second then got hit in the head on a throw while running home. If you haven't seen this, you gotta youtube it.

335. Michael Vick was drafted by the Rockies in 2000 despite not playing organized baseball since 8th grade.

Athletes are athletes.

336. Bobby Bonilla last played for the Mets in 1999 but the Mets still pay him about $1.19M every July 1st from 2011-2035.

He'll be 72 in 2035.

337. Jon Lester played 9 seasons with the Red Sox & 6 seasons with the Cubs. He finished with a .636 W-L% & a 3.64 ERA for both teams.

Well the Cubs knew exactly what they were getting.

338. 4 strikeouts in an inning has occurred 91 times in MLB history.

So how that happens is if strike 3 is a passed ball or in the dirt, the hitter can run to first. This is still insane how often this happens cuz not only does the hitter have to make it to first, but the pitcher has to strike out 4 hitters!

339. The Marlins have won the World Series twice, but still have never won a division title.

And they won each World Series when only 1 wildcard team made the playoffs.

340. Nolan Ryan won 0 Cy Young Awards & recorded 7 no-hitters. Roger Clemens won 7 Cy Young Awards & recorded 0 no-hitters. *

How tf did Nolan Ryan win ZERO Cy Young Awards!?

341. In the 2019 World Series, the road team won all 7 games.

I thought home field advantage was important.

342. For the first 147 seasons of MLB, there were always more hits than strikeouts in each season. For 2018,19,20,21 & 22 there were more strikeouts than hits.

Cool stat to show that the game is changing.

343.The Tampa Bay Rays made the World Series in 2020 with a starting lineup that made a combined $12.5 million in salary that year.

They faced the Dodgers in that World Series. Clayton Kershaw alone had a salary of $16M that year.

344.The Pirates 2021 team salary was $29,479,506. For the 2021 season, 14 MLB PLAYERS had a salary higher than that.

Hmm wonder why the Pirates haven't been good recently.

345. The Twins have lost 18 straight playoff games.

- Swept 0-2 by Astros in 2020
- Swept 0-3 by Yankees in 2019
- Lost wildcard game to Yankees in 2017
- Swept 0-3 by Yankees in 2010
- Swept 0-3 by Yankees in 2009
- Swept 0-3 by Athletics in 2006
- Won Game 1 of ALDS but then lost 3 straight to the Yankees.

346. On 9/25/20, the Marlins clinched a playoff spot to end a 16-year drought.

José Fernández (No. 16) passed away on 9/25/16.

347. The Yankees have won the World Series (27) more often than they've finished the season under .500 (21).

Not bad for a team who's been in the league since 1903. The last time they finished under .500 was 1992. They were under .500 for 4 years in a row then (1989-1992).

348. In MLB history, 4 Pitchers have thrown a no-hitter in their first career start:

1891: Ted Breitesten
1892: Bumpus Jones
1953: Bobo Holloman
2021: Tyler Gilbert

349. No right-handed hitter has ever hit a HR directly into McCovey Cove (SF park).

This means without bouncing in & obviously while the right-handed batter is hitting right-handed.

350. John Smoltz has been teammates with someone on a World Series roster every year from 1982-2021. *

The streak is finally over. What a run.

- **1982** - Ted Simmons with Brewers (Smoltz's teammate on 1988 Braves)
- **1983** - Ozzie Virgil with Phillies (Smoltz's teammate on 1988 Braves)
- **1984** - Darrell Evans with Tigers (Smoltz's teammate on 1989 Braves)
- **1985 & 1987** - Terry Pendleton with Cardinals (Smoltz's teammate on 1991-94, '96 Braves)
- **1986** - Danny Heep with Mets (Smoltz's teammate on 1991 Braves)

- **1988** & **1989** - Walt Weiss with A's (Smoltz's teammate on 1998-2000 Braves)
- **1990** - Norm Charlton with Reds (Smoltz's teammate on 1998 Braves)
- **1991**, **1992**, **1995**, **1996** & **1999** - Self with Braves
- **1993** - Terry Mulholland with Phillies (Smoltz's teammate on 1999-2000 Braves)
- **1994** - Strike, no Series
- **1997** - Marquis Grissom with Indians (Smoltz's teammate on 1995-96 Braves)
- **1998** - Mike Stanton with Yankees (Smoltz's teammate on 1989-95 Braves)
- **2000** & **2001** - David Justice with Yankees (Smoltz's teammate on 1989-96 Braves)
- **2002** - Kenny Lofton with Giants (Smoltz's teammate on 1997 Braves)
- **2003** - Chris Hammond with Yankees (Smoltz's teammate on 2002 Braves)
- **2004**, **2007** & **2013** - David Ortiz (Smoltz's teammate on 2009 Red Sox)
- **2005** - Willie Harris with White Sox (Smoltz's teammate on 2007 Braves)
- **2006** & **2011** - Albert Pujols with Cardinals (Smoltz's teammate on 2009 Cardinals)
- **2008** - Rocco Baldelli with Rays (Smoltz's teammate on 2009 Red Sox)
- **2009** - Mark Teixeira with Yankees (Smoltz's teammate on 2007-08 Braves)
- **2010** - Jeff Francoeur with Rangers (Smoltz's teammate on 2005-08 Braves)
- **2012** - Octavio Dotel with Tigers (Smoltz's teammate on 2007 Braves)
- **2014** - Tim Hudson with Giants (Smoltz's teammate on 2005-08 Braves)

- **2015** - Kelly Johnson with Mets (Smoltz's teammate on 2005-08 Braves)
- **2016** - Jon Lester with Cubs (Smoltz's teammate on 2009 Red Sox)
- **2017**, **2020** & **2021** with Astros, Rays, Braves - Charlie Morton (Smoltz's teammate on 2008 Braves)
- **2018** - David Freese with Dodgers (Smoltz's teammate on 2009 Cardinals)
- **2019** - Josh Reddick with Astros (Smoltz's teammate on 2009 Red Sox)

351. **In the year that Hank Aaron (no. 44) passed away, the Braves won 44 games before the All-Star break, 44 games after the All-Star break, & won the World Series on the 44th week of the year.**

Little extra craziness on this one:
- Braves beat Milwaukee in the 1st round which is where Hank started & finished his career.
- Braves beat the Dodgers in ALCS which is the team Hank hit his record-breaking 715th HR against.
- Braves beat the Astros, coached by Dusty Baker, in the World Series. Dusty Baker was teammates with Hank and he was actually on deck when Hank Aaron hit his 715th HR.

352. The Brewers have only made the playoffs 8 times in their 53 years of existence. All 8 times, they lost to the team that made it to the World Series.

1981 - Lost to Yankees in ALDS, Yankees lost WS
1982 - Lost to Cardinals in WS
2008 - Lost to Phillies in NLDS, Phillies won WS
2011 - Lost to Cardinals in NLCS, Cardinals won WS
2018 - Lost to Dodgers in NLCS, Dodgers lost WS
2019 - Lost to Nationals in NLWCG, Nationals won WS
2020 - Lost to Dodgers n NLWCS, Dodgers won WS
2021 - Lost to Braves in NLDS, Braves won WS

353. During the 2021 MLB season, the Rays used 158 different batting orders & never used the same one more than 3 times.

The first time they used the same batting order in back-to-back games was in the playoffs.

354. In 2021, the Mets set an MLB record for the most time spent in 1st place (103 days) while still finishing the season with a losing record (77-85).

They were 48-40 at the all-star break then went 29-45 after the all-star break.

355. In 1920 & 1921, 2 players both named George Burns won the World Series. Exactly 100 years later in 2020 & 2021, 2 players named Will Smith won the World Series. *

George Burns & Will Smith are also the names of very prolific actors.

356. On 5/10/2022, the right-handed hitter Anthony Rendon took his first at-bat left-handed and hit a HR. *

A 411-foot HR too!

357. On 5/15/2022, the Reds threw a combined no-hitter... they lost 1-0. *

Just when you think it can't get any more embarrassing, it was against the Pirates.

358. On 4/27/2017, the Cardinals beat the Blue Jays on a walk-off grand slam in extra innings. The next time they would play would be 5/23/2022, where the Cardinals won on a walk-off grand slam in extra innings. *

Same poop, different toilet.

359.Christian Yelich is 1 of 5 players since 1901 to hit for the cycle 3 times in his career. ALL 3 TIMES were against the Reds.

As if hitting for the cycle 3 times wasn't crazy enough.

360. *
Vladimir Guerrero Sr.: 87 HRs & .363 OBP in his first 403 MLB games

Vladimir Guerrero Jr.: 87 HRs & .363 OBP in his first 403 MLB games

Like father, like son

361.On 6/15/2022, the Astros became the first team in MLB history to have 2 immaculate innings in the same game. They did it against the same 3 BATTERS! *

For those who don't know, an immaculate inning is defined as an inning where all 3 batters struck out on just 3 pitches. 9 pitches, 3 strikeouts. Ok now that you know this, read this stat again… WTF!

362. On 8/4/22, the Angels hit 7 HRs and lost 8-7. *

Hahahahahahahahahahahahahaha

363. *

On 5/2/2006, Adam Wainwright struck out Craig Biggio.
On 7/27/2022, Adam Wainwright struck out Cavan Biggio.

We know Nolan Ryan struck out lots of father-son combos, but the fact that someone is still doing this in the modern era is remarkable.

364. Matt Olson currently has the longest active streak without missing a game (296 games). He'd have to play every game until 2036 to tie Cal Ripken Jr.'s record (2,632 games). *

Can't wait to update this stat in the 16th edition of this book for Matt Olson breaking the record.

365.On 7/16/2022, Cubs pitcher Michael Givens recorded 2 losses & gave up 0 earned runs. *

He's the first player since 1913 to lose 2 games on 1 day without allowing an earned run.

*1913 was the first season earned runs were tracked

366.On 8/10/22, Cardinals AA prospect Chandler Redmond hit for the HR CYCLE (solo HR, 2-run HR, 3-run HR, & Grand Slam) in 4 consecutive innings. *

As if this wasn't crazy enough to just do this in a game, but FOUR CONSECUTIVE INNINGS!? WTF

367.Buck Showalter has won Manager of the Year in 4 different decades with 4 different teams. *

1994 - Yankees
2004 - Rangers
2014 - Orioles
2022 - Mets

368.Aaron Nola has thrown 19,280 pitches in his MLB career. Of those 19,280 pitches, 9 of them have been 96 mph or more. Of those 9, 3 of them were against his older brother Austin Nola. *

You think those at-bats meant a little bit more?

369.The Yankees franchise has a W-L% of .570 (10,602-8,000) while the Marlins & Rockies have never even finished a single season with a W-L% of .570 or better. *

The Marlins best record was in 1997 (92-70, .568)
The Rockies best record was in 2009 (92-70, .568)

370.The actual play time in an MLB game is about 17 minutes & 58 seconds.

Someone should post these 17-minute highlights on YouTube for every game. I would but it's too much work.

371.If you took every MLB player in history (20,272), there wouldn't be enough players to fill even HALF of the seats at Wrigley Field (20,825). ⋆

The MLB has been around since 1876!!

372.In the Mariners' 46 years of existence, they've experienced just as many ruptured testicles (5) as playoff appearances (5). ⋆

If this stat doesn't make you say WTF, you're reading the wrong book.

373.The iPod was released on 10/23/2001 & officially discontinued on 5/10/2022. During that 20+ year period, the Mariners made the playoffs 0 times. ⋆

The Mariners' playoff drought outlasted the iPod. Luckily the playoff drought finally ended this last season.

374.Not only did Matthew Stafford & Clayton Kershaw play on the same little league team growing up, but they both won their first championship in their 13th career season while playing for Los Angeles. *

Pretty wild huh?

375.The White Sox finished the 2022 season with a record of 81-81. They were 46-46 in the first half of the season, 35-35 in the second half. They had a record of .500 28 different times that season! *

1-1, 6-6, 13-13, 14-14, 15-15, 16-16, 17-17, 18-18, 19-19, 20-20, 21-21, 22-22, 23-23, 33-33, 45-45, 46-46, 48-48, 49-49, 50-50, 51-51, 56-56, 63-63, 66-66, 67-67, 68-68, 76-76, 80-80, 81-81

Oh yeah they're also 9,032-9,032 in their last 18,064 games.

376.All the Astros players involved in the cheating scandal got suspended for a combined total of 0 games.

Absolutely absurd stat.

COLLEGE BASEBALL STATS

377. **2022 was the 75th College World Series. Texas has played in over half of them (38).** *

For those who don't know, the College World Series isn't just 2 teams, it's the final 8 teams. Still, this stat is insane.

378. **On 5/9/1999, Florida State 2B Marshall McDougall went 7 for 7 with 6 HRs & 16 RBIs in a 26-2 win vs. Maryland.** *

That's the NCAA record for the most HRs & RBIs in a game.

379. **On 2/20/21, freshman Caleb Pendleton hit 2 grand slams in his first 2 collegiate plate appearances for Florida Atlantic.**

And if that isn't crazy enough, both grand slams were in the same inning!

380. On 2/09/2021, USCB threw a combined no-hitter with 6 different pitchers, but they still gave up 7 runs & 15 walks.

At least they still won 11-7 despite having 6 errors.

381. In the span of 3 games, Kennesaw State outfielder Josh Hatcher hit for the cycle TWICE. *

Once on 3/23/22 vs. Georgia Tech and again on 3/26/22 vs. North Florida.

382. On 6/3/2022, 2 players in 2 different games BOTH hit a HR from both sides of the plate in the SAME INNING. *

Bryson Worrell of ECU hit a HR from both sides of the plate in the 3rd inning vs. Coppin State & Cole Foster of Auburn hit a HR from both sides of the plate in the 1st inning vs. Southeastern Louisiana.

383. On 6/5/2022 in an NCAA Tournament Elimination Game, Oklahoma State was down 12-0 and won 29-15. *

This was the most runs ever scored in an NCAA Tournament game.

SOCCER STATS

384.In 1964, the 18-year old Tommy Ross scored a hat-trick in 90 seconds.

A hat-trick is 3 goals by the way.

385.Gary Lineker played 567 career games over 16 years but never got a yellow card.

Talk about discipline. Don't think anything like this will ever happen again.

386.Rogério Ceni scored 131 goals during his career. He was a goalkeeper.

Look I don't know much about soccer either if you can't tell from the lack of soccer stats in this book, but I do know that this is absurd.

387.At age 13, Ronaldinho's team won 23-0. He scored all 23 goals.

WTF

388. Jose Mourinho didn't lose a single home league match from March 2002 to April 2011 (125 wins, 25 draws).

Jose Mourinho was the head coach of Porto, Chelsea, Inter Milan, & Real Madrid during this time span.

389. On 2/20/2022 in the Women's SheBelieves Cup, New Zealand defender Meikayla Moore scored a hat trick of own goals vs. USA. *

Meikayla Moore 5' (OG), 6' (OG), 36' (OG).
Then she got benched in the 40th minute.

NHL STATS

390.If you took away all of Wayne Gretzky's career goals (894), he would still be the NHL's all-time leader with 1,983 points.

In hockey, Points = Goals + Assists

391.Together, Wayne & Brent Gretzky hold the NHL record for the most combined points by 2 brothers (2,861).

Brent scored 4. Wayne scored 2,857

392.On 3/23/1952, Billy Mosienko scored a hat trick (3 goals) in a span of 21 seconds.

I don't even think I could do this on an empty net with 3 pucks right in front of me.

393.When he retired, Wayne Gretzky held or shared 61 official NHL records.

Now he holds/shares 60 official records.

394.There were 6 brothers from the Sutter family who played in the NHL from 1982-87.

If that's not crazy enough, they each had 1 son who was drafted into the NHL too.

395.For 20 straight seasons (1980-81 season to 2000-01), only 3 different players led the NHL in points: Wayne Gretzky, Jaromír Jágr, & Mario Lemieux.

Wayne Gretzky led 10 of those years, Mario Lemieux led 6, & Jaromír Jágr led the last 4 years.

* Does not include the 1994-95 season which was shortened by lockout but Jaromír Jágr was tied for the lead.

396.As an NHL rookie in the 1992-93 season, Teemu Selänne scored 76 goals. Only 3 players in NHL history have ever scored more than 76 goals in a season.

- Wayne Gretsky (92 in 1981-82 season & 87 in 1983-84)
- Brett Hull (86 in 1990-91)
- Mario Lemieux (85 in 1988-89)

397.On 4/10/2010, the Boston Bruins scored 3 short-handed goals in 64 seconds.

A short-handed goal is a goal scored when a team's on-ice players are outnumbered by the opposing team's. Normally, a team would be outnumbered because a penalty incurred

398.The Flyers are the only team in the 4 major pro sports (NFL, NBA, MLB, NHL) to alternate making & missing the playoffs for 10 straight years.

2011-12: Made playoffs
2012-13: Missed playoffs
2013-14: Made playoffs
2014-15: Missed playoffs
2015-16: Made playoffs
2016-17: Missed playoffs
2017-18: Made playoffs
2018-19: Missed playoffs
2019-20: Made playoffs
2020-21: Missed playoffs

399. There's been 9,223 different players to play in the 105 year history of the NHL. Patrick Marleau has played with 33% (3009) of them. *

*these numbers are from before the 2022-2023 season but you get the point.

400. 2022 was the first time since 1979 that the Stanley Cup Finals didn't feature at least one of Jaromír Jágr's current or former teammates. *

What's even crazier is only in 1986 & 2021 did a former teammate of his not win it all.

1980: Brian Trottier (1990-1994 Pittsburgh)
1981: Brian Trottier (1990-1994 Pittsburgh)
1982: Brian Trottier (1990-1994 Pittsburgh)
1983: Brian Trottier (1990-1994 Pittsburgh)
1984: Mark Messier (2004 NY Rangers)
1985: Mark Messier (2004 NY Rangers)
1986: Joe Mullen (1990-1997 Pittsburgh)
1987: Mark Messier (2004 NY Rangers)
1988: Mark Messier (2004 NY Rangers)
1989: Jiří Hrdina (1990-1992 Pittsburgh)
1990: Mark Messier (2004 NY Rangers)
1991: Jagr in the final
1992: Jagr in the final
1993: JJ Daigneault (1996-1997 Pittsburgh)
1994: Mark Messier (2004 NY Rangers)
1995: Tom Chorske (1999-2000 Pittsburgh)

1996: Scott Young (1990-1991 Pittsburgh)
1997: Doug Brown (1993-1994 Pittsburgh)
1998: Doug Brown (1993-1994 Pittsburgh)
1999: Benoit Hogue (2002 Washington)
2000: Scott Gomez (2007-2008 NY Rangers)
2001: Chris Drury (2007-2008 NY Rangers)
2002: Brendan Shanahan (2006-2008 NY Rangers)
2003: Jay Pandolfo (2013 Boston)
2004: Pavel Kubina (2012 Philadelphia)
2005: Exclusion
2006: Mark Recchi (1990-1992 Pittsburgh)
2007: Shawn Thornton (2013 Boston a 2015-2017 Florida)
2008: Andreas Lilja (2011-2012 Philadelphia)
2009: Petr Sykora (2006 NY Rangers)
2010: Kris Versteeg (2017-2018 Calgary)
2011: Mark Recchi (1990-1992 Pittsburgh)
2012: Willie Mitchell (2015-2016 Florida)
2013: Jágr in the final
2014: Willie Mitchell (2015-2016 Florida)
2015: Kris Versteeg (2017-2018 Calgary)
2016: Matt Cullen (2006-2007 NY Rangers)
2017: Matt Cullen (2006-2007 NY Rangers)
2018: Alex Chiasson (2012-2013 Dallas)
2019: Brayden Schenn (2011-2012 Philadelphia)
2020: Braydon Coburn (2011-2012 Philadelphia)
2021: Brett Kulak (2017-2018 Calgary)

401.From 1975-1987, Doug Jarvis played in 964 consecutive games (NHL record).

I'm willing to bet this probably won't be broken.

402. **During his NHL career, Joel Rechlicz spent just as much in time in the penalty box (105 min.) as he did on the ice (105 min.).**

So in hockey, there used to be players whose primary purpose of them being on the roster was to get onto the ice and just hit people. Not as popular now.

403. **Bobby Orr was born during Gordie Howe's 2nd NHL season. By the time Gordie Howe retired, Bobby Orr was already in the NHL Hall of Fame.**

Take your time to read this a couple times. You're probably sitting on the toilet anyways.

Also, a player has to be retired a minimum of 3 years before being eligible to enter the Hall of Fame.

404. **Before winning the Stanley Cup in 2019, the St. Louis Blues appeared in 3 Stanley Cups in a row (1968, 1969, & 1970).**

   They got swept all 3 times.

The Buffalo Bills of hockey.

405. In 2017-18, the Coyotes started the season 0-10-1, then claimed goalie Scoot Wedgewood on waivers and in his first game, the Coyotes got their first win of the season.

In 2021-22, the Coyotes started the season 0-10-1, then claimed goalie Scoot Wedgewood on waivers and in his first game, the Coyotes got their first win of the season.

Hm I guess history does repeat itself.

406. On 5/15/2022, the Toronto Maple Leafs became the first team in MLB/NBA/NHL history to lose a winner-take-all game in the opening round of the playoffs 5 years in a row. *

Absolute heart-breaker… 5 YEARS IN A ROW!

407. The Calgary Flames have lost 13 straight Game 2's dating back to the 2004 Stanley Cup. *

For those who like to partake in gambling, you know what to do when the Flames are playing in a Game 2. You're welcome.

408.In 2021, Artturi Lehkonen clinched a trip to the Stanley Cup Finals with a goal in OT.

In 2021, Artturi Lehkonen clinched a trip to the Stanley Cup Finals with a goal in OT. *

He's actually the 2nd player in NHL history to do this. Gordie Drillon did this too in 1938 & 1939

409.From 2020-2022, Corey Perry lost int he Stanley Cup Finals all 3 years with a different team. *

2020: Dallas Stars lost to Tampa Bay Lighting
2021: Montreal Canadiens lost to Tampa Bay Lighting
2022: Tampa Bay Lighting lost to Colorado Avalanche

410.**In 2009, the Avalanche drafted Matt Duchene (1st Rd), Ryan O'Reilly (2nd Rd), & Tyson Barrie (3rd Rd).**

In 2022 on their way to winning the Stanley Cup, the Avalanche beat Matt Duchene's team (Predators) in the 1st round, Ryan O'Reilly's team (Blues) in the 2nd round, & Tyson Barrie's team (Oilers) in the 3rd round of the playoffs. *

Just like a good Thanksgiving dinner, this may be a lot to digest so take your time. Read this stat again if you need to because it's insane!

TENNIS STATS

411.At the 2010 Wimbledon, John Isner & Nicolas Mahut played a match that took 11 hours & 5 minutes over 3 days.

The total of 183 games beat the previous record of 112 games.

412.Rafael Nadal is 112-3 in his career at the French Open. *

He has 14 French Open titles. From 2005-2020, there were only 3 years where he didn't win it (2009, 2015 & 2016).

413.Roger Federer holds the record for the most consecutive Grand Slam Final appearances with 10.

He also has the 2nd most with 8.

414.50% of Roger Federer's name is "er".

Facts are facts, don't hate.

GOLF STATS

415. Byron Nelson won 11 straight PGA tournaments in 1945.

Tiger's best was only 7 straight.

416. From 1997-2008, Tiger Woods was a combined 126 UNDER par in the majors.

The second best during that span was 63 OVER par (Joe Ogilvie).

417. Tiger Woods won the 1997 Masters by 12 strokes.

12!

During that same 1997 Masters tournament, Tiger Woods set 20 Masters records & tied another 7 records.

418.Since the Official World Golf Rankings began in 1986, only 4 golfers have won a major championship while being ranked number 1. 3 of those golfers have only done it once. Tiger Woods has done it 11 times.

Ian Woosnam - 1991 Masters
Fred Couples - 1992 Masters
Rory McIlroy - 2014 PGA Tour
Tiger Woods - 11 times

419.The youngest players to win the US Women's Open:

2008 - Inbee Park (19 years, 11 months, 7 days old)

2021 - Yuka Saso (19 years, 11 months, 7 days old)

420.Phil Mickelson has won 3 of the 4 majors. The only one he's missing is the U.S. Open where he's finished 2nd, 6 different times.

He's won the Masters 3 times, PGA Championship twice, & The Open Championship once.

421. The longest putt ever made on television (159 ft) was made by none other than, Michael Phelps.

Yeah like the swimmer. I guess this kind of makes sense because who else is putting from 53 yards out.

422. On 8/6/2021, Cameron Smith tied the PGA Tour record by only putting 18 times in a full 18-hole round.

Now only 9 golfers have done this.

NASCAR STATS

423.Ryan Blamey has 2 wins at Talladega. Both times he won by .007 seconds.

Insane that we can even measure time to that low of a decimal.

424.Alex Bowman finished in every position (2nd-43rd) in the Cup Series before finally finishing 1st.

Love both of those but that's enough NASCAR stats.

425.On 7/24/22, Chase Elliot won at Pocono despite not leading a single lap. *

I'm gonna be honest here. I don't know much about NASCAR so I don't know how often this happens but this seems pretty crazy to me.

TOM BRADY STATS

426. Tom Brady is older than 13 of the 32 (41%) NFL head coaches. *

Tom Brady is 45. The following coaches are all younger than 45: Kliff Kingsbury (43), Arthur Smith (40), Zac Taylor (39), Kevin Stefanski (40), Nathaniel Hackett (42), Matt LaFleur (43), Brandon Staley (39), Sean McVay (36), Mike McDaniel (39), Kevin O'Connell (37), Robert Saleh (43), Nick Sirianni (41), Kyle Shanahan (42).

427. As a Buccaneer, Tom Brady has thrown 71 TDs & 0 INT in the Red Zone. *

Not bad for an old man.

428. 2022 was the first time in Tom Brady's 23-year NFL career that his team was 2 games under .500. *

Ok that's just crazy. What the actual f***

429.In their pro careers, Tom Brady has a better chance of making the Super Bowl (45.5%) than Steph Curry has making a 3-pointer (42.8%). *

I know what you're thinking, "You can't compare those!" And I say just like apples & oranges, they can absolutely be compared.

430.In between Tom Brady's 7th & 22nd NFL season, Calvin Johnson got drafted, retired, & inducted into the Hall of Fame.

In the NFL, a player must be retired for at least 5 years before being eligible to be voted into the Hall of Fame.

431.In between Tom Brady's 1st & 7th Super Bowl win, Troy Polamalu got drafted, had a 12-year career & got inducted into the Hall of Fame. *

Even with 1 year to spare.

432. Tom Brady has played in 10 Super Bowls but only twice has his team scored in the 1st quarter.

It wasn't until his 8th Super Bowl when his team finally scored in the 1st quarter. They scored 3 points in the first quarter of Super Bowl LII where they lost to the Eagles & 7 points in the first quarter of Super Bowl LV where they beat the Chiefs.

433. Tom Brady has more playoff wins (34) than the Washington franchise (23) that's been around since 1932.

You know it's crazy when you compare a player to a FRANCHISE.

434.Since Tom Brady entered the NFL (2000) he's had a higher chance of making the Super Bowl (45.5%) than 8 teams had of just winning a regular season game. *

*Tom Brady has made the Super Bowl 10 out of 22 seasons. The 2022 season is not included.

Team	Win % since 2000
Cardinals	44.2%
Jets	44.1%
Texans	42.4%
Washington	41.9%
Raiders	40.2%
Jaguars	36.9%
Lions	34.9%
Browns	33.5%

435.In 2002, Tom Brady became the youngest starting QB to win a Super Bowl.
In 2021, Tom Brady became the oldest starting QB to win a Super Bowl. *

He been the GOAT from the beginning.

436.Super Bowl LVI was the 10th time the starting QB of the Super Bowl was named "Joe". This tied the record with "Tom" for the most Super Bowl QB starts which were all Tom Brady. *

Well, Tom Brady might just be better than your average Joe.

437.Tom Brady has more Super Bowl MVPs (5) than losses to the Bills (3) in his career.

Tom Brady is 32-3 (.914) vs. the Bills. The best win percentage vs. one team in NFL history.

438.Tom Brady has NEVER lost 3 division games in the same season. *

Over 23 seasons where you have 6 regular season division game a year, that's pretty impressive.

439.Tom Brady has thrown more TD passes since turning 40 (182) than Rich Gannon (180), Steve McNair (174), Troy Aikman (165), Daunte Culpepper (149), & Michael Vick (133) did in their entire CAREER. *

This doesn't even include postseason!

440.Tom Brady has thrown more TD passes since turning 30 (491) than Aaron Rodgers has thrown in his entire career (470). *

This also doesn't include postseason!

441.Before the 2022 season, Tom Brady has only lost more than 2 games in a row once in his career (2002). *

He lost 3 games in a row in 2022 but still... WTF

442.Before that 3-game losing streak, Tom Brady had 302 consecutive starts without a 3-game losing streak. The next closest QB to do that was Joe Montana with 155 consecutive starts without a 3-game losing streak. *

Why do I feel like it's always Joe Montana's records Brady keeps breaking?

443.28 pro sports championships have occurred while Tom Brady was living in that area/city.

Year	Brady's location	Team	Success
1980	N. California	Raiders	Super Bowl
1981	N. California	49ers	Super Bowl
1984	N. California	49ers	Super Bowl
1988	N. California	49ers	Super Bowl
1989	N. California	49ers	Super Bowl
1989	N. California	Athletics	World Series
1994	N. California	49ers	Super Bowl

1995	Michigan	Red Wings	Con. Champions
1996	Michigan	Red Wings	Stanley Cup
1997	Michigan	Red Wings	Stanley Cup
1998	Michigan	Michigan BB	Nat. Champions
2001	Michigan	Red Wings	Stanley Cup
2001	New England	Patriots	Super Bowl
2003	New England	Patriots	Super Bowl
2004	New England	Patriots	Super Bowl
2004	New England	Red Sox	World Series
2007	New England	Red Sox	World Series
2007	New England	Patriots	Super Bowl
2008	New England	Celtics	NBA Champ
2011	New England	Bruins	Stanley Cup
2013	New England	Red Sox	World Series
2014	New England	Patriots	Super Bowl
2016	New England	Patriots	Super Bowl
2018	New England	Red Sox	World Series
2018	New England	Patriots	Super Bowl

2020	Tampa Bay	Lightning	Stanley Cup
2021	Tampa Bay	Buccaneers	Super Bowl
2021	Tampa Bay	Lightning	Stanley Cup

444. Tom Brady is not the only player that was drafted in the 6th round, won a Super Bowl in his 2nd season and was born August 3rd.

Those are all true for Tyrod Taylor as well.

445. In the 10 seasons from 2010 to 2019, Tom Brady & the Patriots had a win streak of at least 6 games during the regular season every year except 2013 (still went 12-4). *

The Jaguars didn't even have a single 6-game win streak in that 10-year span.

446. Tom Brady has more career wins than the Buccaneers' previous 28 starting QBs combined.

This man won a Super Bowl with one of the historically worst franchises in the NFL in just one season. Wtf.

447. Tom Brady has more playoff wins (35) than 28 NFL franchises. *

Only NE, GB, & PIT have more. The 49ers also have 35.

448. Tom Brady has more than twice as many playoff wins (35) as any other QB in NFL history. *

Tom Brady: 35
Joe Montana: 16

449. Tom Brady has twice as many Divisional Round wins (14) as any other QB in NFL history.

Joe Montana is 2nd with 7.

450. Joe Montana is the only QB who has more TOTAL playoff wins (16) than Tom Brady has in the Divisional Round ALONE (14).

I'm starting to think I could write an entire book on just Tom Brady stats.

451.Tom Brady has twice as many Super Bowl appearances (10) as any other QB.

The 2nd most is John Elway with 5.

452.Tom Brady has won more Super Bowls (7) than any other player has even played in.

The 2nd most is his former kicker, Stephen Gostkowski with 6 & former Bills & Broncos DT Mike Lodish with 6.

453.Tom Brady has made 13 consecutive playoff appearances (NFL Record). The last time Tom Brady missed the playoffs (2008). Instagram didn't even exist yet. *

Could easily be 14 straight playoff appearances by the time you're reading this.

454.Tom Brady is the oldest player to ever play in a Super Bowl. No other QB has started a Super Bowl after age 40. He's done it 3 times.

Tom vs. time, even Tom wins that battle.

455. Tom Brady is 3-1 in the playoffs when throwing 3 or more interceptions.

During the Super Bowl era, all other QBs are 20-123 when throwing 3+ interceptions.

456. Tom Brady has more career passing yards (87,571) than Joe Montana & Steve Young combined (73,675).

This just doesn't sound right but it is.

457. Tom Brady's 21 Super Bowl TD passes only total for 159 passing yards while Kurt Warner's 6 Super Bowl TD passes total for 174 yards. *

AND 33% of Kurt Warner's Super Bowl TD passes were only 1 yard passes!

458. Brady has an NFL-record 3,039 career passing yards in the Super Bowl, more than twice as many as any other player in league history.

Kurt Warner is second with 1,156 yds.

459. **Tom Brady's record in championship games (conference championships & Super Bowls):**

1-5 vs. Manning brothers
16-2 vs. everyone else

Wonder what his records would be if the Manning family never existed.

MICHAEL JORDAN STATS

460. Michael Jordan is the only NBA player who has scored at least 15 points in every playoff game of his career.

He played in 179 career playoff games.

461. In a 32-month span, Michael Jordan won 3 championships, 3 scoring titles, 2 MVPs, & 3 Finals MVPs all without missing a single game.

That was from November of 1995 to June of 1998.

462. After losing the first 3 games of the 90-91 season, Michael Jordan never lost 3 games in a row again as a Bull.

Including playoffs, he played 626 games in that span.

463.From Nov. 1995 - June 1997, the Bulls were the favorite to win in 185 consecutive games.

Who was betting against the Bulls during those days anyways.

464.While on the Bulls, Michael Jordan faced 983 different opponents. He outscored 982 of them head to head in points per game.

Only Allen Iverson outscored him 27.1-24.0 PPG.

465.Michael Jordan started off his pro baseball career with a 13-game hit streak.

He batted a .327 during that streak.

466.In MJ's first 11 seasons, he won the scoring title 10 times.

He didn't win it in his rookie year. He got 3rd with 28.8 PPG.

WILT CHAMBERLAIN STATS

467.During his 14-year NBA career, Wilt Chamberlain never fouled out of a game.

Pretty impressive for someone who averaged 45.8 minutes per game in his career.

468.Wilt Chamberlain scored 100 points in a game.

What kind of sports stats book would this be if this wasn't included?

469.Wilt Chamberlain is the only player in NBA history to score 50 or more points AND 40 or more rebounds in a game.

He did it 5 times.

01/25/1960: 58 pts & 42 reb vs. Pistons
01/21/1961: 56 pts & 45 reb vs. Lakers
12/08/1961: 78 pts & 43 reb vs. Lakers
10/26/1962: 50 pts & 41 reb vs. Pistons
11/22/1964: 50 pts & 40 reb vs. Pistons

470.During the 1961-62 NBA season, Wilt Chamberlain averaged 50.4 PPG & 25.7 RPG.

He did not win MVP that year.

Bill Russell won it with 18.9 PPG & 23.6 RPG

471.On 11/24/60 in a game vs. Bill Russell & the Celtics, Wilt Chamberlain grabbed 55 rebounds.

The Celtics entire team only had 59 rebounds that game yet still beat the Warriors 132-129.

472.In the 1961-62 season, Wilt Chamberlain played 4,458 minutes out of a possible 4,466 minutes.

He only missed those 8 minutes because he was ejected.

473. During the 1961 season, Wilt Chamberlain averaged more minutes per game (48.5) than there are minutes in regulation (48).

The .5 comes from games he played in that went to overtime.

474.On 2/2/68, Wilt Chamberlain had 22 points, 25 rebounds, & 21 assists.

A double-triple-double?

475.Only 3 times in NBA history has a player averaged over 38 points per game in a season. All 3 times were Wilt Chamberlain.

He didn't win MVP any of those years.

476.Wilt Chamberlain is in the volleyball hall of fame.

The International Volleyball Association was short lived, but he was also the president. Not a bad retirement hobby.

MISCELLANEOUS STATS

477.In the NFL, NBA, MLB & NHL, the team that holds the record for the most wins during the regular season did not win the championship that year.

NFL: 2007 Patriots (16-0), lost Super Bowl
NBA: 2015-16 Warriors (73-9), lost NBA Finals
MLB: 1906 Cubs (116-36), 2001 Mariners (116-46).
NHL: 1995-96 Red Wings (62-13-7), 2018-19 Lightning (62-16-4)

478.A 3-peat champion has occurred 10 times in the NBA, 9 times in the NHL, 7 times in MLB, but NEVER in the NFL.

Tom Brady is still playing so this could change.

479. On 5/25/1935, Jesse Owens broke 5 world records in 45 minutes at the Big 10 Championship track meet.

He was also injured during this track meet. He needed assistance getting in and out of his car from falling down the stairs 5 days before the meet. His coach almost pulled him out of the race before the meet began.

480. As a college wrestler, Cael Sanderson went 159-0 with 4 NCAA D1 individual titles.

Well I guess this proves the "no such thing as perfect" theory wrong.

481. During the 7 years where Lance Armstrong won every Tour de France (1999-2005), 87% of the top-10 finishers (61/70) were confirmed or suspected dopers.

Just a crazy stat that the media didn't want you to know at the time.

482.If Michael Phelps were a country, he'd rank 35th in all-time gold medals (25), ahead of 107 nations.

Man, it'd be kind of weird if Michael Phelps was a country though…

483.Olympic judo champion, Teddy Riner, went 154-0 over a span of 9 years.

Again, thought there was no such thing as perfect…

484.On 5/11/2010, Tommy Golick bowled 47 straight strikes.

That's 1 strike away from 4 full games worth of strikes.

485.As a high school head coach, John Beam didn't lose a single regular season game in the 90's.

Yes this is the coach from Last Chance U.

486. Kansas State & Virginia Tech are the only Power 5 schools who have NEVER won a national championship in a team sport.

Currently, there's 65 Power 5 schools & 8 official team sports.

487. Steve Nash & Julio Jones are the same height (6'3")

This one just doesn't sound right. Shows how tall NBA players are.

488. Derrick Henry: 6'3" 238 lbs
Donald Trump: 6'3" 243 lbs

Ok last stat like this, too great to not put in the book.

489. Jahangir Khan won 555 consecutive squash matches in tournaments from 1981-1986.

I guess no matter how obscure or common the sport is, somebody has absolutely dominated everyone at some point.

490.In 2019, Eliud Kipchoge became the first person to ever run a marathon in under 2 hours (1:59:40). That's a pace of 4 min. 34 sec. per mile.

Really read this one again, and keep in mind how fast you ran just 1 mile at your peak athletic ability. Reminder: a marathon is 26.2 miles

491.2020 was the first time EVER that one city (Los Angeles) won 2 major pro sports championships in the same calendar month.

Thank you COVID-19 for making this bizarre stat possible for the Lakers & Dodgers.

492.On 6/4/21, Montana Fouts became the first pitcher in 21 years to throw a perfect game at the Women's College World Series.

She recorded those perfect 21 outs on her 21st birthday.

493.On 4/11/21, North Texas softball pitcher Hope Trautwein pitched a perfect game where she struck out every single batter.

21 strikeouts in 7 innings.

494.Carolina Panthers LB Shaq Thompson has made over $35M in guaranteed salary money so far in his NFL career. But before he played in the NFL, he played minor league baseball for the Red Sox organization when he was 18. In his pro baseball career, he went 0 for 39 with 37 strikeouts.

I know what you're thinking, "Even I could do that." And you actually might be right. Safe to say Shaq Thompson made the right career choice.

495.Only one city has won 3 major sports titles in the same sporting year. The crazy part is that it's Detroit!

1935-36 season (MLB, NFL, & NHL)

496.Aaron Judge was a 3-sport athlete in high school. Here were his numbers: *

Football (TE): 54 rec   969 YDs   17 TDs
Baseball (1B/P): .500 BA   7 HRs   32 RBIs
                pitching: 9-3 W-L   0.65 ERA   65K
Basketball (C): 18.2 PPG 12.8 REB per game

497.Floyd Mayweather made more money in 24 minutes in his fight vs. Logan Paul ($100M) than Michael Jordan made playing in the NBA for 15 seasons ($90M). *

I know there's a little inflation that's not accounted for but 24 minutes vs. 15 years... WTF!

498. *

8/29/2001: Serena Williams wins at US Open, Albert Pujols hits a HR, and Vlad Guerrero Sr., Craig Biggio, & Dante Bichette all record a hit.

8/29/2022: Serena Williams wins at US Open, Albert Pujols hits a HR, and Vlad Guerrero Jr., Cavan Biggio, & Bo Bichette all record a hit.

This is nuts. 21 years apart, a couple legends are doing the same exact thing while some legends' offspring are doing the same thing… wtf

499.Jim "Mattress Mack" McIngvale earned an estimated $75 million payout (largest in sports betting history) when the Astros won the 2022 World Series. *

He had $10 million in bets on the Astros to win the World Series.

500.Is eating hot dogs a sport? Well here's the most hot dogs consumed in 10 minutes at the Annual Nathan's Hot Dog Eating Contest: *

Name	Year	Hot Dogs
Joey Chestnut	2021	76
Joey Chestnut	2020	75
Joey Chestnut	2018	74
Joey Chestnut	2017	72
Joey Chestnut	2019	71
Joey Chestnut	2016	70
Joey Chestnut	2013	69
Joey Chestnut	2012	68
Joey Chestnut	2009	68
Joey Chestnut	2007	66

BIBLIOGRAPHY

If you're reading this, I'm sure you're looking to see the sources for each stat. Well, you'll be disappointed. I'm only one person and there's no way I was putting together a full bibliography in MLA, APA, or whatever dumb format they forced us to learn in school.

I will say, that just like the WTF Stats Instagram page, every single stat is verified by some legitimate source. Most stats are verified through sports-reference.com or one of their pages specific to a sport. I pride myself on the work I put into this book and can personally guarantee every single stat is true to the best of my knowledge at the time of writing this book. You'd be surprised how often you see stats on the internet that are false or impossible to verify. There's a lot of stats I had in the first draft of this book that I had to remove for that reason.

Anyways, I hope you enjoyed this book. I put a lot of time and effort into perfecting it, but if for some reason you didn't enjoy it or you believe something in this book was misleading or offensive, then get over it.

23664091R00105